Institutions, Inflation and Unemployment

To Duda and Thomaz

Institutions, Inflation and Unemployment

Edward J. Amadeo

Associate Professor
Department of Economics,
Pontifícia Universidade Católica
do Rio de Janeiro (PUC/Rio)

Edward Elgar

Published by
Edward Elgar Publishing Limited
The Lypiatts
15 Lansdown Road
Cheltenham
Glos GL50 2JA
UK

Edward Elgar Publishing, Inc.
William Pratt House
9 Dewey Court
Northampton
Massachusetts 01060
USA

British Library Cataloguing in Publication Data

Amadeo, Edward J.
   Institutions, Inflation and Unemployment
   I. Title
   332.41

Library of Congress Cataloguing in Publication Data

Amadeo, Edward J.
   Institutions, inflation and unemployment / Edward J. Amadeo.
   200p. 22cm
   Includes bibliographical references and index.
      1. Inflation (Finance)—Brazil.   2. Indexation (Economics)—
   –Brazil.   3. Wages—Government policy—Brazil.   I. Title.
   HG835.A63   1994
   332.4'1'0981—dc20   94–16369
                                                            CIP

ISBN 978 1 85278 682 3

Printed on FSC approved paper
Printed and bound in Great Britain by Marston Book Services Ltd, Oxfordshire

Contents

Acknowledgements

This book is the outcome of years of work with my colleague José Márcio Camargo. We have tried to put together an analysis of the Brazilian recent economic performance in which distributive conflict and institutions, in particular unions and wage bargaining, play an important part in understanding the chronic and creeping characteristics of inflation.

As well as with José Márcio, other friends and colleagues helped me in writing this book. The work of Stephen Marglin on growth and distribution and the ideas of Lance Taylor and Amitava Dutt on distribution, inflation and capacity utilization are at the root of the macroeconomic model of Chapter 4. The views of Jaime Ros on distributive conflict and inflation were essential for the development of the theoretical apparatus of Chapters 2 and 3. Finally, the work of Bob Rowthorn on corporatism provided the initial impulses for the schemes developed in Chapter 5.

Three institutions helped me in writing the book. The department of economics at the Pontificia Universidade Católica in Rio de Janeiro, where I work, has a unique environment for the development of academic research in Brazil. The Kellog Institute at the University of Notre Dame, where I spent the first semester of 1991, working with Amitava Dutt, contributed with a congenial atmosphere for my work. Finally, a grant from the Center for Latin American Studies at the University of Pittsburgh allowed me to concentrate on the book.

Among my students in Rio I wish to thank Marcello Estevão for his keen assistance. Marcelo Guimarães and Simone Passini, also my assistants, showed that even facing the troubled economic and social situation in Brazil the young can have great initiative and responsibility.

I wish to thank Mr Edward Elgar who is publishing my third book in English. It is terribly difficult for those living in developing countries to publish in the Northern Hemisphere. The encouragement of Mr Elgar has been an essential input for my academic career and that is why I am profoundly thankful to him. The work of Mrs Julie Leppard and the editorial staff at Edward Elgar Publishing Ltd are responsible for making my style

vi

reasonably acceptable to English speakers.

My wife Eduarda helped me with the mathematics in Chapters 2 and 3. But our love and the birth of our child Thomaz were certainly the best parts of the years I worked on the book.

List of Figures and Tables

Figures

Tables

1. Introduction

Themes

A close examination of cases of rampant inflation will show that they end up in explosive processes. This does not seem to be the case in Brazil during the 1980s and early 1990s. The monthly rate of inflation in that period suffered astonishingly rapid accelerations, oscillated between 0 and 80%, and yet did not explode without limits as in the classic cases of hyperinflation in Germany and Hungary after the First World War, or the recent case of Bolívia. It is as if there were perennial pressures determining the growth of prices and wages coexisting with countervailing forces limiting the extent to which inflation accelerates.

Living with high and erratic rates of inflation has damaging effects for an economy even if explosive situations do not arise. A small forecasting error can develop into a tragedy. A 2% under estimation of the monthly rate of inflation implies a 27% error in twelve months. The probability of incurring such errors in an environment of very volatile rates of inflation is quite significant. Income and wealth losses are frequent. Depending on the indexation scheme, asset holders and wage earners may experience significant losses in periods of acceleration of the rate of inflation, and that is why in many countries there is a flight into foreign currencies to protect their wealth. This flight into foreign currencies and goods is the first important step towards hyperinflation. The fact that the yield of government bonds as well as a significant range of prices, wages and incomes are indexed to inflation in Brazil is another important factor in reducing the possibility of explosive hyperinflation.

Changes in the inflationary regime due to significant moves in relative prices or a price freeze are associated with major distributive shifts. However, these types of shifts are sporadic. Another type of distributive shift arises even in the case of smooth processes of acceleration of inflation when the adjustment of money incomes of certain agents continuously lag behind the increase in prices. Because it is subtle and sometimes imperceptible to agents, inflation serves as a hidden mechanism to redistribute income. A

1

redistribution which might seem unthinkable through open negotiation between the relevant parties (due to political or ethical reasons) becomes possible under the veil of inflation. Hence, situations of unresolved distributive conflicts may survive for a long period without open confrontation or hostilities. Perhaps this is the notion behind Hirshman's observation that 'inflation ... is a remarkable invention that permits a society to exist in a situation that is intermediary between the extremes of social harmony and civil war' (1985, p. 201).

Governments play an important role in this process. Varied mixes of monetary, fiscal and exchange rate policies affect inflation in such a way that the net effect on the distribution of income is not at all clear to the economic agents in the private sector.

An attempt to deal with the theme of inflation and distributive conflict must have as a starting point the ancient notion of class conflict or social conflict. In a society, social groups have common as well as conflicting objectives. In simple terms, the common objective is to increase the 'wealth of the nation' whereas the conflicting objectives refer to the division of the wealth. It is possible to imagine situations in which the disputes associated with the conflicting objectives preclude the development of a *modus vivendi* compatible with the achievement of the common objective. However, to deal with the relation between common and incongruous objectives is too hard a task. To simplify, we can think of a situation in which the wealth of the nation is given, and there is a dispute over the shares and the absolute sums going to each of the social groups.

A possible way to go ahead with this exercise is to imagine a situation in which all social groups are happy with their respective shares and sums, and then assume a change in the environment which reduces the total wealth. The groups must now share the losses. The simple loss of income – given the shares – might lead to a situation of distributive conflict. If the shares remain constant no one is really poorer, in relative terms. But in comparison with the past, everyone feels poorer. An attempt to reduce the level of poverty translates into an attempt to change the shares, and that is when the distributive conflict starts.

The attempt to become richer by agent 'j' manifests itself through an increase in the price of the good or service she supplies to the market, or in an attempt to change relative prices in her favour. There are two circumstances in which the attempt to become richer may fail. Depending on the elasticity of demand for the good produced by agent j, her total income might increase or shrink. If the agent optimizes her income given the technological and market constraints, there are no good reasons for believing that she was not optimizing before the shock. Hence, there are no good reasons to believe that she would be able to increase her income by increasing her price.

The other restriction comes from inflation. If other agents increase their prices to recover the loss incurred due to the increase in the price of good j, the effect on the real income of agent j will gradually fade away. In this sense, inflation works as an escape valve through which the discontent of the agents flows, neutralizing their initial efforts to increase the purchasing power of their income.

The role of indexation schemes is to protect the agents' income against inflation. When the rate of inflation is volatile, the incomes of the agents become volatile too unless automatic indexation schemes exist. The extent to which wages or prices are indexed to inflation depends on the size of the indexation factor itself and on the period of adjustment. With 20% monthly inflation, if the period of adjustment is three months and the monthly income of an agent is $100, the total income loss (compared with a situation of zero inflation) is of the order of $89. In real terms, instead of earning $300 in three months the agent will earn $211. The shorter the period of indexation, the smaller the income loss. If the period was one month, the loss over three months would be of the order of $50.

In a situation of pervasive indexation in which all prices and wages were perfectly indexed to inflation, inflation would be harmless. Inflation would be distributive-neutral. However, indexation is never pervasive. Indexation periods vary across sectors of the economy and there is always the possibility of an inflationary shock which affects different agents in different ways. In an environment of volatile rates of inflation, the capacity of agents to forecast the future path of inflation is very small. Given that there are transaction costs associated with price and wage negotiations, agents try to be as parsimonious as possible and avoid recurrent negotiations.

There are two possible ways to avoid recurrent negotiations.

One is to establish automatic adjustments of prices or wages. In the relation between clients and suppliers this implies a clause to adjust prices every '*n*' months; in the case of firms and unions, it implies a clause to adjust wages every '*m*' months. Hence, indexation and the shortening of the indexation period is the first response to unstable inflation or as a protection against the acceleration of inflation in the future.

A second and radical response to the possibility of an inflationary spur in the future is to increase prices or wages more than the increase in past inflation. We refer to this phenomenon as 'overindexation' of past inflation. When all agents – or those agents with sufficient market power – start overindexing their prices and wages, the result is an acceleration of inflation. This is a typical case of self-fulfilling expectations. When a number of agents react to the possibility of an acceleration of inflation by overindexing past inflation, the result is the acceleration of inflation. This is what in Latin America economists call 'defensive inflation'.

When all major agents in the economy behave defensively and overindex past inflation, it becomes very difficult to stop the acceleration of inflation. Two possible responses are: an orthodox aggregate demand policy to reduce the market power of agents or a heterodox approach based on a price and wage freeze. Both alternatives were implemented in Brazil during the 1980s and early 1990s. Neither worked – at least until 1993 when this book was written. Orthodox policies do not work because the indexation of prices and wages is insensitive to demand contractions. Heterodox policies fuel inflationary forces by creating a misalignment of relative prices and relative wages. After more than a decade of acceleration of inflation and numerous attempts to stabilize the economy, the conflict over the distribution income has given rise to an environment of rampant uncertainty. The common goal of the agents – that is, to create wealth – has surrendered to the disarray fostered by inflation and distributive conflict.

Under these conditions, the situation reaches a point in which not even those who gained from inflation think that inflation is functional any longer. The defensive behaviour of the agents gives rise to a situation in which there are no coordinating forces capable of promoting the end of inflation and the resumption of economic growth.

The story just told is one of the relation between distributive conflict and inflation in an environment of pervasive uncertainty. There are institutional aspects of the contract between employers and employees which make this story even more plausible. The aim of this book is to tackle the role of these institutions in the Brazilian experience with inflation.

The key notion in the connection between institutions and inflation is the coordination of the processes of price and wage formation. There is a growth in the dispersion of relative prices and wages when some agents overindex their prices in anticipation of an acceleration of inflation. The obvious response of those who did not overindex their prices or wages is to try to at least index them to the new rate of inflation. This of course establishes a new level of the 'core' inflation. One may think of a situation in which, after a realignment of prices and wages to the 'anticipation shock', relative prices and wages return to the initial level. No one gained from inflation, and yet from a systemic perspective, the acceleration of inflation hurt the whole community. This is a typical situation in which coordinating mechanisms in the formation of prices and wages would help.

A wage law or a price freeze are both examples of coordinating mechanisms. They might not work if they lack credibility, that is, if agents think that there are groups who are not following the rule or if they believe that the rule will not prevail in the future.

Wage laws and price freezes are government policies. There are other types of coordinating mechanisms. Institutional arrangements which affect negotiations between clients and suppliers and between firms and unions are very important in this connection. In particular, the institutional organization of wage bargains – that is, the timing of wage negotiations and the grouping of bargaining parties (firms and unions sitting around the same bargaining table) – may have an important impact on the formation of expectations and on the attitudes of the agents. Defensive price increases in anticipation of future inflationary spurs result from the lack of information about the behaviour of other prices and wages in the economy. In this sense, an argument can be made in favour of the existence of 'pattern setters' and the synchronization of bargains in order to increase the level of information and reduce the defensive drives.

Structural factors can also affect the behaviour of agents. Market constraints impose limits on the capacity of firms to increase their prices, and by extension on the capacity of unions to increase wages. Hence, the levels of domestic and international competition have an effect on the attitudes of agents in fixing their prices. The structure of the Brazilian economy and the institutional basis of wage bargains do not create a congenial environment for price stability. On top of the structural and institutional base, a series of economic and political factors help to explain the development of the inflationary crisis of the 1980s and early 1990s.

Brazil has a very closed economy (imports are only 5% of GNP) and the industrial structure is very concentrated. Hence, market restrictions are not very tight. Wage negotiations are scattered over the year and the degree of centralization of bargains is very low. As a result, pattern setters do not exist and, in the face of an inflationary environment, the incentives to protect wages against future shocks by overindexing past inflation are enormous.

The external debt crisis led the Brazilian government to devalue the domestic currency in 1979 and again in 1983. The 'overindexation' of the exchange rate implied a change in relative prices which the 'new union movement' born with the democratization process was not prepared to accept. The result was the accommodation of the distributive conflict involving the government, firms and workers through the rapid acceleration of inflation in the first half of the 1980s. In the second half, a series of heterodox stabilization experiments based on price and wage freezes increased the disorder which was already established in the price system. Such disorder, together with the uncertainty associated with the future path of inflation, led the economic agents to incorporate a defensive attitude and gave rise to recurrent waves of wage and price overindexation.

Organization of the Monograph

This monograph navigates from the abstract to the concrete. It starts with economic schemes and models, goes through an examination of institutional approaches to the organization of unions and the structure of wage bargains and ends up with a discussion of the relation between unions, wage bargains and inflation in Brazil.

Chapter 2 starts with a presentation of the arithmetic of the

Introduction

relation between inflation and real wages, introducing the
backbones of the models developed in Chapters 3 and 4. We
emphasize the roles of the length of the adjustment period and the
size of the indexation factor of wages with respect to past inflation
in the determination of the real wage. After establishing the
concepts of overindexation and distributive dissatisfaction, we show
that the expectation of an acceleration of inflation increases the
distributive dissatisfaction of workers creating incentives to
overindex past inflation.

The other task of the chapter is to establish the arithmetic of the
relation between overindexation and inflation. Such a relationship
is not independent of the 'size' of the bargaining party. We show
that the greater the number of firms and workers involved in a
negotiation (or the greater the size of the bargaining party), the
stronger the effect on inflation of an increase in wages and prices.
This is simply the result of the process of aggregation of prices
leading to the average price level. This is a simple but important
result for it highlights the connection between the level of
centralization of wage bargains and the impact of wage increases
on the aggregate rate of inflation.

In Chapter 3 we discuss the factors affecting the attitude of
unions in wage bargains. We assume that unions choose the degree
of indexation of wages by maximizing the difference between the
benefit and costs of increasing money wages. The benefit is
associated with the increase in the peak real wage, or the wage
immediately after the negotiation. The costs are associated with the
sacrifices imposed by the firms on workers during conflictive
bargains and the indirect effect of overindexation on the real wage
through the increase in inflation. Here is where the centralization
of bargains plays an important role in affecting the attitude of
unions. We show that the greater the centralization of bargains, the
stronger the indirect negative effect of overindexation on the real
wage and hence the greater the reasons for wage moderation on
the part of unions. We also examine the effect of changes in the
length of the indexation period and the tightness of market
restrictions on the behaviour of the unions.

The model developed in Chapter 3 is based on a partial
equilibrium framework. In particular, it takes as given the level of
activity and the level of employment both in the industry and in the
economy as a whole. In Chapter 4 we present a model which takes

7

into account the role of changes in real wages (or the distribution of income) on aggregate demand, and thus integrates the determinants of wages and prices with the determinants of the level of activity. The model was tailored to discuss the workings of alternative stabilization approaches. We show that orthodox demand management policies can only work by producing an increase in unemployment and real wages, and that heterodox plans based on price and wage freezes may be incompatible with the macroeconomic equilibrium. Furthermore, we argue that the acceptability on the part of unions of negotiated incomes policies hinges on the relation between the distribution of income and the level of aggregate demand and employment. In particular, if wage moderation results in falling real wages and growing unemployment, the carrots for the unions to participate in the pact simply do not exist.

Chapter 4 discusses the political science literature on the factors affecting wage moderation. It is, in a sense, the institutional counterpart of the models developed in the previous chapters. The themes are the same, the arguments are very similar, but the language is different. We look at the institutional basis of wage bargaining in purely pluralist and corporatist social structures and then suggest the existence of hybrid or intermediary cases. Our conclusions are in line with those advanced by Calmfors and Driffill (1988), according to which intermediary situations are not conductive to wage moderation. We then extend the analysis to construct a taxonomy of stabilization approaches in the face of different systems of wage bargaining.

Chapter 6 starts looking at the Brazilian case. We examine the evolution of the union movement with special emphasis on the rise of the new-unionism of the 1980s, exploring its social profile, main ideas and views with respect to wage bargaining. We then examine the structure of wage bargaining in Brazil and conclude that it has many of the attributes of the hybrid cases depicted in Chapter 5. Hence we identify some of the rooted factors behind the inflationary process in Brazil. Finally we examine the development of the stabilization crisis and identify as a symptom of it the gradual lack of adherence of the evolution of wages to the wage law.

Chapter 7 starts with an empirical evaluation of the macroeconomic crisis and its impact on the labour market. It shows the evolution of aggregate employment, the structure of employment between the formal and informal segments of the labour market and the distribution of income. The second part of the chapter tries to apply some of the notions developed in the theoretical and conceptual chapters to an analysis of the evolution of relative wages and prices in the Brazilian industrial sector. The interesting result is that in most industries, there exists a positive correlation between relative wages and prices over time. We suggest that this might be seen as evidence that the attitude of firms in wage bargains is affected by the competitive conditions of their respective markets.

2. Inflation and Real Wages

Introduction

In an economy with high inflation, real wages oscillate dramatically. Wage laws and private arrangements between unions and firms reduce the impact of price increases on the purchasing power of wages through periodical adjustments of money wages to past inflation. Inevitably, however, between two wage adjustments, real wages fall. With 20% monthly inflation for example – something not unusual in Latin American countries during the 1980s – if wages are adjusted to past inflation every three months, the real wage will fall more than 40% over the adjustment period.[1]

In an economy with high and volatile inflation, every month, hundreds of wage bargains take place and hundreds of thousands of firms have to make price decisions. Transaction costs preclude bargains between unions and firms and among suppliers and clients from taking place every week or month. Wages and prices are adjusted periodically, but not in a synchronous fashion. The fact that wage bargains are spread over the year reduces the level of information on the future path of inflation. Changes in the conditions of the economy affect in different ways the bargaining power of unions negotiating over the year. A union negotiating today has enormous difficulties in forecasting the impact on inflation of wage bargains of other labour groups in the future.

For each agent in the economy, the higher the level of inflation and the longer the period of adjustment of its price, the greater the risk of incurring losses if the actual rate of inflation exceeds the expected rate. Thus, bargains over the wage and over the pattern of wage adjustments between negotiations tend to be complicated and difficult for both firms and unions.

When the rate of inflation is not only high but also irregular, the task of the unions trying to guess the path of inflation becomes even harder. The level of uncertainty – or the inability to form a probabilistic guess about the future course of inflation – increases with the variance of inflation. There are many factors affecting the variability of inflation in economies with high and chronic inflation.

Public tariffs and the exchange rate often lag behind inflation thus leading to fiscal and balance of payments difficulties in the face of which the government is forced to promote major adjustments, thus affecting the path of inflation. Price freezes, usually followed by inflation spurs, also augment the variability of the rate of inflation. All these factors contribute to make the wage bargain process very difficult and time demanding. This is why unions are constantly trying to shorten the adjustment period of automatic wage adjustments in order to reduce the risks of suffering unexpected wage losses and the need to enter into new negotiations. For the same reasons, the attitude of unions in wage bargains tends to be quite different from their attitude in economies with low and stable rates of inflation.

In an environment of accelerating inflation and uncertainty about the degree of acceleration, the incentives for wage moderation are virtually none. Indeed, in the face of recurrent accelerations of the rate of inflation in the past and an uncertain future, unions try to overindex past inflation in an attempt to defend wages against future accelerations of the rate of price increases.[2] However, the overindexation of wages itself creates inflationary pressures through its effects on costs. If prices are indexed to changes in costs, the immediate result of wage overindexation is an acceleration of inflation. Hence, in a sense, the uncertainty about the future path of inflation gives rise to an 'inflationary attitude' on the part of unions – and indeed on the part of all economic agents.

In this and the following chapter we examine the relation between inflation and real wages. In Chapter 3, we shall pay special attention to the factors affecting the behaviour of unions during wage bargains. We will stress the role of the institutional environment in which wages are negotiated with special emphasis given to the degree of centralization of wage bargaining.

The present chapter presents the backbones of the model developed in Chapter 3. It starts with a simple model which establishes the arithmetic of the relation between inflation and real wages. We study the effects of changes in the rate of indexation of money wages and the length of the adjustment period on the behaviour of real wages over time. Next, based on a simple price equation, we try to capture the effect on inflation of changes in the degree of money – wage indexation under different assumptions on the degree of centralization of wage bargaining. We show that, the greater the degree of aggregation of wage negotiations, the greater the impact on inflation of a given increase in the rate of wage indexation. This result is important if we want to understand the potential effects of the centralization of bargains on the attitude of unions – a central theme of the following chapters.

The Arithmetic of Inflation and Distribution

The model developed in the following pages mimics the pattern of wage bargains and wage adjustment found in most Latin American economies with high inflation. Wages are negotiated once a year and adjusted to past inflation periodically during the year. The length of the indexation period (or adjustment periods) varies from zero (when wages are not adjusted over the year at all) to one month (when wages are adjusted every month) to one week or one day in cases of hyperinflation. Wage laws usually determine the indexation period, but in many cases unions privately negotiate shorter intervals with firms.

The degree of centralization of the wage bargain varies from country to country and, within the same country, from industry to industry. There are countries in which bargains take place at the level of the firm (the US is the best example), others in which they take place at the industry level or sectoral level (as in most European countries), and others in which negotiations take place at the national level (as in the Northern countries of Europe). In what follows we will be thinking of a case in which negotiations are decentralized and scattered over time, that is, in which they are not synchronized. However, the level of decentralization might differ from industry to industry.

In order to provide a simple and rigorous analysis of the relation between inflation and the path of real wages over time, let us assume that, over a year, the monthly rate of inflation is constant. During the year, wages are automatically adjusted to inflation N times. The 'period of adjustment' – that is, the interval between two automatic adjustments – is given by $\psi = 1/N$. If, for example, wages are adjusted three times a year, the 'period of adjustment' is equal to $\psi = 1/3$ of a year, that is, four months.

The illustration below shows the case in which wages are adjusted three times a year. As noted already, we assume that, in each industry, the money wage is negotiated between unions and firms once a year, and over the year, wages are fully adjusted to inflation at the end of every adjustment period (t+ψ, t+2ψ, and t+3ψ). For example, if monthly inflation is 20%, and the adjustment period is four months, at the end of the fourth month the money wage will be automatically adjusted to 52% to recover the peak level attained immediately after the negotiation.[3] At the end of the third indexation interval, unions and firms negotiate the annual adjustment of wages. Such adjustment can be smaller or greater than past inflation depending on the bargaining power of the union.

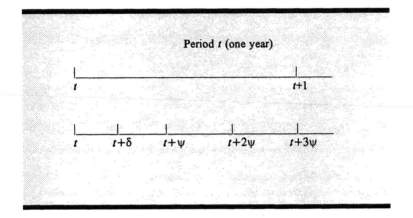

Illustration 2.1

Assuming constant inflation, and making $\delta \equiv \psi/2$, we can write:

$$\frac{P_{t+\psi}}{P_{t+\delta}} = \frac{P_{t+\delta}}{P_t} \qquad (2.1)$$

where $P_{t+\tau}$ is the price level in t+τ where τ can be zero, δ or ψ. If wages in sector j of the economy are negotiated in the beginning of the year, say at t, the 'peak real wage', that is, the maximum real wage immediately after the negotiation, will be given by the ratio between the money wage ($W_{t,j}$) and the price level in t (P_t):

$$\omega_{t,j}^{P} = \frac{W_{t,j}}{P_t} \qquad (2.2)$$

The 'average real wage' over the adjustment period, that is, over ψ, will be given by the ratio between the money wage negotiated in t and the price level in the middle of the adjustment period, that is, the price level in $t+\delta$ $(P_{t+\delta})$:

$$\omega_{t,j} = \frac{W_{t,j}}{P_{t+\delta}} \qquad (2.3)$$

Using equations (2.1) to (2.3), we can write the average real wage as a function of the peak real wage (2.4)

$$\omega_{t,j} = \omega_{t,j}^{P}\left(\frac{P_t}{P_{t+\delta}}\right) \qquad (2.4)$$

According to equation (2.4), the average real wage depends on the peak wage and the rate of inflation as given by the ratio $P_t/P_{t+\delta}$. With constant inflation, the annual rate of inflation P_t is given by:

$$1 + p_t = \left(\frac{P_{t+\psi}}{P_t}\right)^N = \left(\frac{P_{t+\delta}}{P_t}\right)^{2N} = \left(\frac{P_{t+\delta}}{P_t}\right)^{1/\delta}$$

which obviously implies:

$$(1+p_t)^{\delta} = \left(\frac{P_{t+\delta}}{P_t}\right) \qquad (2.5)$$

Replacing (2.5) in (2.4) gives:

$$\omega_{t,j} = \frac{\omega_{t,j}^{P}}{(1+p_t)^{\delta}} \qquad (2.6)$$

14

We now have the real wage as a function of the peak real wage, the rate of inflation in year t and the length of the adjustment period.

The Wage Curve

When negotiating money wages, unions attempt to recover the purchasing power losses of wages incurred due to inflation since the last bargain or to protect the purchasing power of wages against an acceleration of inflation in the following year. With automatic and complete indexation over the year and constant inflation, workers will not incur any loss. However, if we consider the possibility of an unexpected acceleration of inflation during the past year or a situation in which indexation is incomplete, there might be a loss to be negotiated in the annual wage bargain. On the other hand, even with constant inflation and complete indexation, if the union has reasons to believe that inflation will accelerate in the future, or if there is uncertainty as to the future path of inflation, the annual negotiation becomes an important instrument to protect the purchasing power of the real wage in the ensuing year.

In a competitive environment, workers only get their 'reservation wage', independently from the path of labour productivity. However, if there exists a positive relationship between productivity and wages – as argued in the 'efficiency wages' literature for example – or if unions have any type of monopolistic power (as they usually do), firms are sensitive to unions' demands associated with productivity gains. When this is the case, the path of labour productivity becomes an important factor in determining money wages. Hence, in general, unions bargain to recover real wage losses (or to prevent future losses) and, in addition, they bargain over real increases in wages due to changes in labour productivity. We assume that unions negotiating with firm(s) j try to adjust the wage according to the following equation:

$$W_j^d = W_{-1j} [1 + \lambda_j^d(p_{-1} + \zeta_{-1j})] \qquad (2.7)$$

W_j^d is the desired wage and λ_j^d stands for the desired indexation factor, p_{-1} is the rate of inflation of the consumer price index (CPI) since the last bargain and $\zeta_{-1,j}$ is the rate of variation of productivity over the last 12 months. According to the equation, unions try to 'index' the money wage negotiated 12 months ago ($W_{-1,j}$) to the rate of price inflation and to changes in labour productivity. The size of the desired indexation factor, λ^d_j, depends on the levels of organization and militancy of the union members, on the degree of dissatisfaction of workers with their real wage and on the expected rate of acceleration of inflation.[4] The *ex post* indexation factor, or the effective 'bargaining power of the union', λ_j, depends on the determinants of λ^d_j, on the one hand and, on the other, on factors associated with the bargaining process. We shall return to the determinants of the actual indexation factor in Chapters 3 and 4. For the moment, let us take it as a given.

The actual indexation factor is at most equal to the desired indexation, $\lambda^d_j \geq \lambda_j$, and the actual variation of the wage between t-1 and t, that is, during year t-1, is given by

$$w_{-1,j} = (\frac{W_{t,j}}{W_{-1,j}}) - 1 = \lambda_j v_{-1,j} \qquad (2.8)$$

where $v_{-1,j} = (p_{-1} + \zeta_{-1,j})$. Note that whenever $\lambda_j > 1$, given the rate of inflation, *real* wages will grow faster than productivity in which case we say that there is overindexation of wages. If, on the other hand, $\lambda_j < 1$, there is 'underindexation', and real wages will be falling in relation to productivity growth.

The inflationary process and the associated distributional implications are critically influenced by the size of the indexation factor of money wages with respect to the changes in consumer prices and productivity. The overindexation of wages is certainly an important factor in processes of acceleration of inflation. Indeed, if prices are indexed to changes in costs, an overindexation of wages will lead to an acceleration of the rate of inflation. It is important to realize that the overindexation of wages is not necessarily associated with an increase in real wages. Wages might overindex past inflation – and this is the sense in which the concept is used here – but, depending on the path of inflation, it might very well underindex future inflation in which case the real wage will fall. Hence, the overindexation of wages is not inconsistent with falling real wages, as commonly noted in processes of rapid acceleration of inflation.

The Real Wage

We can now derive an equation where the real wage is a function of the indexation factor (λ), the focus of the analysis in the following chapters. Dividing both sides of equation (2.7) by P_t, we can write the peak real wage as a function of the indexation factor:

$$\omega_{t,j}^P = \omega_{-1,j}^P [\frac{(1+\lambda_j\nu_{-1})}{(1+p_{-1})}] \qquad (2.9)$$

Substituting equation (2.9) in (2.6), the real wage becomes a function of the indexation parameter λ_j :

$$\omega_{t,j} = \omega_{-1,j}^P [\frac{(1+\lambda_j\nu_{-1})}{(1+p_{-1})}][\frac{1}{(1+p_t)^\varsigma}] \qquad (2.10)$$

Equation (2.10) says that the average real wage depends on the indexation factor (λ_j), the rate of inflation (p_t) and the adjustment period (δ).There is obviously nothing that unions can do in relation to the course of inflation in the future. They must take p_t as a given. In fact, they must form an expectation of the value of p_t and, as noted already, in economies with chronic and volatile inflation, there is considerable uncertainty with respect to the future rate of inflation. Unions can negotiate with firms over the value of λ and the value of δ.

Figures 2.1 to 2.4 depict the path of the logarithm of the real wage over two years (months 1 to 24) and the average real wage. The annual negotiation takes place at the beginning of month 13, and wages are automatically adjusted to inflation every four months. The higher the rate of inflation, the steeper the curve and the greater the reduction of the real wage during the adjustment period. Figure 2.1 shows the situation in which the indexation factor resulting from the annual bargain between the union and the firm(s) is smaller than 1 ($\lambda= 0.9$). In this case, the wage is only partially indexed to past inflation, and the average real wage will necessarily fall. The reduction in the peak wage negotiated in month 13 determines a reduction in the average real wage, given the rate of inflation and the length of the adjustment period. Figure 2.2 shows the path of the real wage and the average real wage when the indexation factor is greater than 1 ($\lambda=1.1$). The increase in the peak wage in month 13 implies an increase in the average real wage in the second year. In the case where the indexation factor is 1, the average real wage remains constant over the two years.

Figure 2.3 shows the effect over the average real wage of an increase in the length of the adjustment period from 4 months in the first year to 6 months in the second year. The average real wage will fall for a given rate of inflation. Finally, Figure 2.4 depicts the case in which the monthly rate of inflation falls from 20% in the first year to 10% in the second year. The wage curve becomes flatter in the second year determining an increase in the average real wage, given the peak wage and the length of the adjustment period.

Distributive Dissatisfaction

Unions have a certain target or desired real wage. Such a target wage is not arbitrary. It is constrained by certain factors or, otherwise, it would be obviously infinite. The desired wage results from certain conditions affecting the bargaining power of the union among which labour market conditions and capital – labour relations play a prominent role. In a recession, for example, the bargaining power becomes smaller due to the increase in the cost of job loss to workers. Given the determinants of labour demand, the bargaining power of workers also depends on the relation between the real wage and productivity.[5]

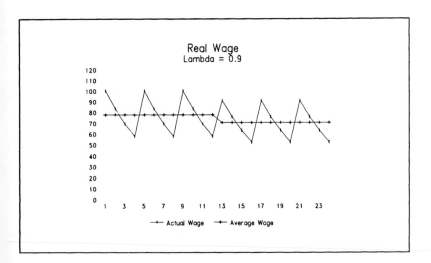

Figure 2.1

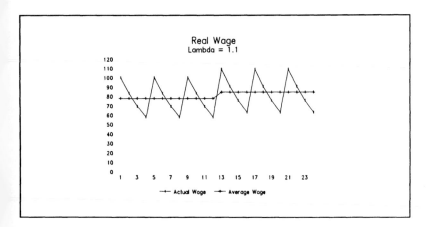

Figure 2.2

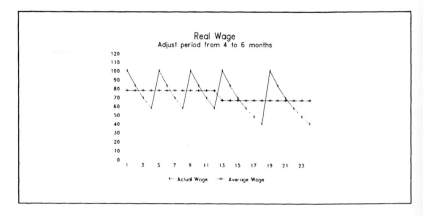

Figure 2.3

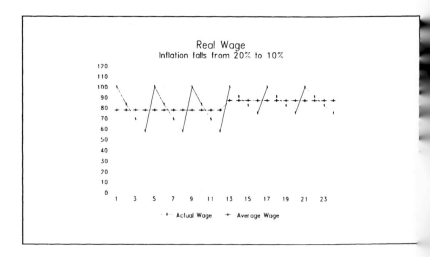

Figure 2.4

Let us call ω^d the target or desired real wage associated with the indexation factor λ^d. A situation of distributive dissatisfaction on the part of workers arises when the real wage (as determined by equation (2.9)) is smaller than the target real wage, that is:

$$\omega^P_{-1,j}[\frac{(1+\lambda_j v_{-1,j})}{(1+v_{-1,j})}][\frac{1}{(1+p_t^e)^\delta}] < \lambda^d$$

We have replaced the rate of inflation in equation (2.9) by the *expected* rate of inflation. Given the target wage, the expected rate of inflation in t (p_t^e) and the indexation period (δ), there exists a level of λ for which $\omega = \omega^d$, that is, the expected real wage equals the target wage. As shown in Figure 2.5, the real wage or the expected real wage (since it is associated with the expected rate of inflation), ω, is a linear function in λ. An increase in the expected rate of inflation or an increase in the length of the adjustment period, shift the ω line downwards. Either one of the modifications require an increase in the indexation factor in order to close the dissatisfaction gap given by $\omega - \omega^d$.

The increase in the indexation factor required to maintain the value of the real wage constant in the face of an increase in the expected rate of inflation is given by:

$$d\lambda_j = \frac{[\delta(1+\lambda_j v_{-1,j})]}{[v_{-1,j}(1+p_t^e)]}dp_t^e > 0$$

Given the expected rate of inflation, there exist a set of combinations of values of the indexation factor and the length of the indexation period associated with the level of the target wage. The locus of pairs λ, δ is depicted in Figure 2.6. The iso-wage curves are positively sloped. It is easy to see why: an increase in the length of the indexation period will reduce the wage and thus require an increase in the indexation factor to restore the original value of the wage. Formally, the slope of the iso-wage curve is given by the derivative:

$$\frac{d\lambda}{d\delta}\Big|_{\omega\ given} = \frac{[(1+\lambda_j v_{-1,j})\ln(1+p_t^e)]}{v_{-1,j}} > 0$$

21

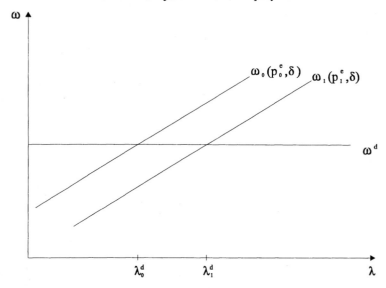

Figure 2.5 The real wage and the indexation factor ($p_1^e > p_0^e$)

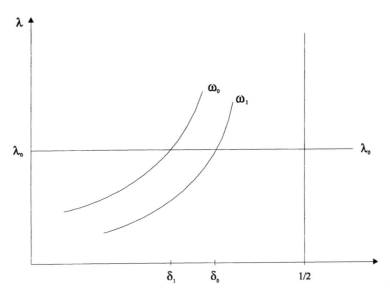

Figure 2.6 The Iso-wage curve ($\omega_0 > \omega_1$)

An increase in the target wage will shift the iso-wage curve downwards implying either an increase in the indexation factor or a reduction in the length of the adjustment period. This discussion highlights the factors affecting the attitude of unions in wage bargains. As noted already, there is nothing unions can do with respect to the rate of inflation, which they must take as a given. The focus of the negotiation must be therefore the indexation factor and the length of the adjustment period. The latter is an object of bargain if the wage law is not binding. That is, if a law fixing the adjustment period (and the automatic adjustment factor) exist, firms and unions cannot negotiate the value of δ. In such case, the only variable left for negotiation is the the yearly indexation parameter λ.

However, the attitude of unions is not independent from the values of the expected rate of inflation and the length of the adjustment period. A new information leading to a revision of expectations or the possibility of a alteration in the wage law will affect the desired level of the indexation factor and thus the attitude of workers and unions.

Price Formation in Industry

We assume that industrial goods markets are not perfectly competitive. Firms have some degree of market power resulting from restrictions to entry or competition in their markets. As a result, the price of goods will usually be greater than the competitive price, and relative prices will be influenced by the degrees of market power of firms.

We assume that firms set a mark-up over direct average costs. The size of the mark-up varies with structural factors (such as barriers to entry, monopoly rights, protection from international competition) as well as short-run fluctuations (such as movements in the elasticity of demand). Firms have both direct labour and non-labour costs, and in each firm, industry or sector, the weight of each of the components in total direct costs varies. The price equation of a typical firm, industry or sector j is given by:

$$\Pi_{t,j} = M_{t,j}[(\frac{W_{t,j}}{\Delta_{t,j}})^{v_j}(\frac{\Pi_t}{\beta_{t,j}})^{1-v_j}] \qquad (2.11)$$

where:

$\Pi_{t,j}$ = wholesale price of good j;
$M_{t,j}$ = profit margin over direct costs;
$W_{t,j}$ = money wage rate;
$\Delta_{t,j}$ = average product of labour;
Π_t = average wholesale price level of industrial goods;[6]
$\beta_{t,j}$ = technical coefficient expressing the ratio of material direct costs per unit of output;
γ_j = share of labour costs in total costs, and
$(1 - \gamma_j)$ = share of material costs.

We shall treat β and γ as given. Immediately after the negotiation with unions, firms decide on the size of the mark-up based on their strategies and market restrictions. We will discuss the role of the latter in the following chapter. Once the mark-up is decided upon, the new rate of inflation of industrial prices, that is, the rate of inflation of year t, is determined. The time derivative of equation (2.11) yields the rate of inflation of the price of good j:

$$\pi_{t,j} = \frac{\Pi_{t,j}}{\Pi_{t,j}} = m_{t,j} + c_{t,j} \qquad (2.12)$$

where $c_{t,j} = \gamma_j\,(w_{-1,j} - \zeta_{-1,j}) + (1 - \gamma_j)\pi_t$ is the rate of inflation of direct costs, $m_{t,j}$ is the rate of change of the mark-up, and all lower-case letters represent the time derivative of the corresponding variables, assuming the time derivatives of β and γ to be zero. We suppose that c_t costs is given by the variation in labour costs over the last 12 months ($\gamma_j\,(w_{-1,j} - \zeta_{-1,j})$) plus the current variation in non-labor costs ($(1-\gamma_j)\pi_t$). The rate of inflation of industrial prices can also be written as:
The variable ε_j measures the degree of indexation of the price level to cost inflation. From equations (2.12) and (2.13) it is clear that

$$\pi_{t,j} = \epsilon_{t,j}\, c_{t,j} \qquad (2.13)$$

whenever $\varepsilon_j > 1$, the mark-up increases, and vice-versa, that is, $m_j > 0$ when $\varepsilon_j > 1$.

Note that, according to equation (2.13), the rate of inflation of industrial prices depends on both the indexation factors of wages with respect to CPI inflation (λ) and of industrial prices with respect to costs (ε).

Inflation

Before we proceed, it is important to emphasize the difference between the relevant rates of inflation for the workers and for the firms, that is, the difference between the relevant rates of inflation for the determination of the *real wage* and the *product wage*. Workers care about the rate of inflation of the consumer price index (CPI) which, together with the money wage, determines the real wage. Whereas firms look at the rate of inflation of wages in relation to the inflation of industrial prices (or wholesale prices) in the determination of the product wage.

In what follows, we will take the CPI rate of inflation as given and concentrate the discussion on the factors affecting the determination of wages and industrial prices. In other words, we will take p_{-1} as given and then study the factors determining w_{-1} and π_{t}, or the wage inflation over year t-1 and the rate of inflation of the wholesale price index in year t, respectively. In what follows, we will derive an equation for the aggregate rate of inflation of industrial prices. For convenience, a 'sector' will be defined as a set of productive units which negotiate together with a single union. Thus, a sector can be either a single plant, a single firm (with more than one plant), a restricted set of firms or all firms in the same industry. A centralization of wage bargains, involving a greater number of firms, increases the size of a 'sector' thus defined, and thus its weight in the price index.

Let α_j be the weight of sector j in the wholesale price index. Hence, the aggregate rate of inflation of wholesale prices will be given by:

$$\pi_t = \Sigma \alpha_j \pi_{t,j} = \Sigma \alpha_j \varepsilon_j c_{t,j} \qquad (2.14)$$

where Σ refers to summation over j, j ranging from 1 to n, and n is the number of sectors or 'bargaining parties' in the economy. Solving for π_t we get equation (2.15):

$$\pi_t = \frac{\Sigma \alpha_j \epsilon_j \gamma_j [\lambda_j \nu_{-1,j} \zeta_{-1,j}]}{[1 - \Sigma \alpha_j \epsilon_j (1 - \gamma_j)]} \qquad (2.15)$$

Hence, the aggregate rate of inflation of industrial prices depends on the indexation factors of wages and prices in all the *n* sectors. The greater these factors the greater will be the rate of inflation. The next step is to study the effect of changes in the indexation factors of wages on aggregate inflation. The question is: what are the elements determining the impact on inflation of an increase in the indexation factor of wages in sector *j*? Differentiating π_t with respect to λ_j gives:

$$\frac{\partial \pi_t}{\partial \lambda_j} = \frac{[\alpha_j \epsilon_j \gamma_j \nu_{-1,j}]}{[1 - \Sigma \alpha_j \epsilon_j (1 - \gamma_j)]} \qquad (2.16)$$

Note that, *ceteris paribus*, the greater the size of the sector (given by α_j), the greater the impact of an increase of λ_j on π_t. This is an obvious but important result. It says that an increase in the indexation parameter of a large sector will have a greater effect on inflation than an increase in the parameter of a small sector. Also, the impact on inflation will be greater the larger the size of the indexation factor of prices (ϵ_j).

The point becomes clearer if we assume that all sectors have the same size, in which case, $\alpha_j = \alpha = 1 /n$. Now, an increase in the number of sectors (*n*) will imply a reduction in their sizes, and vice-versa. The effect of an increase in λ in sector *j* on the average rate of inflation is now given by equation (2.17). Note that the smaller the number of sectors, the greater the effect of an increase of λ_j on π_t. Now, the number of sectors is inversely related to the level of centralization of wage bargains. A large number of sectors implies a large number of bargaining parties and thus a decentralized pattern of wage bargaining. The conclusion derived from equation (2.17) is that the impact on inflation of an increase in the indexation factor will be greater the higher the degree of

$$\frac{\partial \pi_t}{\partial \lambda_j} = \frac{(\epsilon_j \gamma_j \nu_{-1,j})}{n[1 - (\frac{1}{n})\Sigma \epsilon_j (1 - \gamma_j)]} \qquad (2.17)$$

centralization of wage bargains.

Finally, to close the circuit, let us assume that the inflation of consumption goods prices (p) is linearly related to the inflation of wholesale prices (π), say $p_t = v\pi_t$. Given this assumption, it becomes obvious that the rate of CPI inflation over period t is not independent from the bargaining power of unions (λ) on which wages were negotiated at the beginning of the period. To see this we differentiate p in relation to λ:

$$\frac{\partial p_t}{\partial \lambda_j} = v(\frac{\partial \pi_t}{\partial \lambda_j}) \equiv \Theta_j \qquad (2.18)$$

Note that Θ_j is negative in n: the greater the number of sectors, and therefore the smaller the share of each sector in the average price index, the greater the effect of a change in the bargaining power on the rate of inflation.

Conclusion

This chapter was designed to highlight the relationship between inflation and the path of real wages. An important aspect of this relation is the role played by feed-back effects through the indexation of wages to prices and of prices to costs. Pervasive indexation is characteristic of economies with high and chronic inflation. Stable economies also have a certain degree of indexation. But the extent to which it becomes generalized in certain regions, as in some Latin American countries, does play a role in characterizing inflationary-prone economies, and thus deserves special attention.

The interesting thing about indexation is that if it were really pervasive, both the rate of inflation and relative prices and wages would remain stable and generalized over time. In such a situation, indexation would not be particularly harmful. Indexation is harmful only to the extent that it prevents the rate of inflation from falling but, on the other hand, it makes life with inflation possible. Economic agents need a certain degree of indexation depending on the level of inflation. The higher the rate of inflation, the greater the demand for indexation.

The only effect of indexation is to perpetuate inflation, not to accelerate inflation. An acceleration of inflation can result only from an overindexation of prices, that is, from an inflation of certain prices greater than the rate of inflation in the past. Hence, the causes of overindexation are the really important elements in a discussion of the determinants of inflationary processes. Why do agents overindex their prices? The simple answer to this question is that they want to change relative prices in their favour. Now, relative prices do change in stable economies. Why does the rate of inflation not reach explosive levels there? There are a few possible answers to this question.

The first is that market constraints are not as stringent in most Latin American countries as they are in other industrialized or semi-industrialized regions. The high levels of protection of domestic producers against foreign competition was part of the development a strategy in most countries in Latin America. One of the effects of such a strategy was to reduce the pressure on domestic firms to keep prices competitive.

The second answer is that maybe there exists an unsettled distributive conflict or a conflict among economic agents over the distribution of income in inflationary economies. The notion of distributive conflict – to which we will return in Chapter 4 – is very complicated. It involves a discussion on the relative bargaining power of different groups in society and on the reasons for the dissatisfaction of the groups with their share of the pie. However difficult the discussion of the theme might be, it seems unquestionable that the attempt to change relative prices due to a rooted discontent of certain social groups with their current incomes is an important determinant of inflationary processes.

The final answer has to do with uncertainty and transaction costs. There are transaction costs associated with the renegotiation of wages and prices. Hence, agents must be parsimonious in their drive to renegotiate. On the other hand, the volatility of inflation and the uncertainties associated with the future path of inflation create the incentives to increase the degree of indexation. Now, the degree of indexation really has two dimensions: one is the indexation factor and the other is the adjustment period. The limits to the shortening of the length of the indexation period are set by the transaction costs involved in negotiating prices. The greater these costs, the greater the incentives to increase the indexation factor to protect incomes from inflation. This is probably the most important factor determining the incidence of overindexation in inflationary economies.

In this chapter we discussed the relation between inflation and real wages, and introduced the notion of indexation factors of wages and industrial prices. We also established a relationship between the real wage, the peak real wage, the rate of inflation and the length of the indexation factor.

An important result of the exercise was to show that, given the rate of inflation and the duration of the indexation interval, an increase in the adjustment parameter will lead to an increase in the peak wage – or the wage immediately after the negotiation – and that this will have a positive effect on the average real wage over the year. Hence, unions will have an obvious reason to try to increase the indexation factor. However, on the other hand, an increase in the indexation factor will have a positive effect on the rate of inflation, and thus affect negatively the real wage. The effect on inflation will be greater the higher the level of centralization of wage bargains. Hence, in a centralized system of wage bargaining, the incentives to increase the indexation factor of wages become smaller.

Notes

1. That is, if wages are adjusted on January 1ˢᵗ, the purchasing power of wages will be 40% smaller on March 31ˢᵗ, just before a new adjustment.
2. By 'overindexation' we mean a situation in which wages grow faster than prices between two negotiations.
3. In most countries with high inflation, a wage law determines the adjustment period as well as the degree of adjustment of the money wage to past inflation. Where a law does not exist, unions negotiate with firms not only the rate of adjustment of wages but also the adjustment period.
4. The greater the expectation of future inflation, the smaller the expected real wage in the future, and thus the greater the incentives to mobilize to demand wage increases.
5. We have in mind the arguments put forward by the efficiency wages literature as in found in McDonald and Solow (1981) and Shapiro and Stiglitz (1984).
6. The composition of non-labour costs is not discernible from the data-base used for the purpose of the empirical analysis in Chapter 7. That is why it is assumed that in all sectors the composition is the same as the composition of the average industrial price index.

3. Wage Determination in Economies with High Inflation

Introduction

The conventional wisdom on the relation between inflationary processes and income distribution is that the correlation between inflation and real wages is negative. The reason for this is that money wages are usually indexed to inflation with a lag. This, of course, is only a half truth. Some wages are only partially indexed to past inflation and others are fully indexed to past inflation which implies that in both cases (in the first more than in the second) real wages will fall as inflation accelerates. But there are groups of workers whose money wages are overindexed in relation to past inflation, and therefore not only fuel the acceleration of inflation, but may also increase in real terms over time.

In countries or sectors where labour unions are combative and workers are very militant, money wages may grow ahead of inflation. Unions are said to be irresponsible when trying to overindex wages. As the argument goes, unions are actually creating inflationary pressures which eventually will reduce their real wage. If, instead, wage restraint was the rule, the rate of inflation would fall, and the purchasing power of wages would increase. This, again, is only a half truth. If there were a coordinated process of wage determination, in which all wages were adjusted to inflation simultaneously, and if firms agreed to keep their profit margins constant, the rate of inflation would remain constant, and also real wages and wage differentials would remain constant. If, furthermore, firms accepted a reduction in their profit margins, inflation would fall, and real wages would increase. But usually wages are not determined simultaneously (wage bargains are scattered over the year) and firms do not have any commitment with a fixed mark-up – let alone a falling mark-up. Indeed, uncertainty concerning the outcome of negotiations elsewhere in the economy is an essential feature of wage bargains in decentralized systems with significant effects on the behaviour of unions. Usually, not only is the effect of the indexation of wages upon inflation not taken into account by the unions, but even if it was, it could be rational in many circumstances to overindex wages in relation to past inflation. Rational in the sense that it might increase the real wage, or at least protect it from unexpected inflationary shocks.

In this chapter we address the logic of wage determination in a regime of high and accelerating inflation, and the rational basis of overindexation. Unions look at the inflationary effects of overindexation of wages only to the extent that it might reduce their real wages. We will assume that unions face incentives and costs to increase the degree of indexation of wages, and that to the extent to which the marginal benefits are greater than the marginal costs, will the level of indexation increase. If the result of the wage bargain is inflationary, in principle this should not be seen as a concern of the unions. In other words, we do not assume that unions see inflation as bad in itself.

There are a variety of elements, different in nature, affecting the bargaining attitude of unions in wage negotiations. Institutions, market constraints and expectations are all important factors. The central notion, however, is that unions and workers care about the future path of relative wages when bargaining over their wages. This notion was first put forward by Keynes in the *General Theory* where he argued that

> the struggle about money-wages primarily affects the *distribution* of the aggregate real wage between different labour-groups, and not its average amount per unit of employment which depends ... on a different set of forces. The effect of combination on the part of a group of workers is to protect their *relative* real wage". (1936, p. 14)

In Keynes' view, the average real wage depends on the aggregate rate of inflation over which individual unions do not have any control. On the other hand, the distribution of the aggregate wage bill among workers of different sectors depends on the path of relative wages. Keynes is right that in a decentralized system of wage bargaining, unions can only care about their own wage, and that the purchasing power of the latter will depend on the wages of other labour groups.

However, as the level of centralization of bargains and the size of the bargaining parties increase, unions may start to have a sense of the likely effect of their wage demands on aggregate variables and, in particular, the effect over the rate of inflation. If this is indeed the case, the incentives to the union to demand increases in money wages, in an attempt increase the relative wage of the union members, are reduced as the level of centralization of wage bargaining increases. As seen in Chapter 2, the greater the size of the bargaining party, the more stringent becomes the trade-off between the direct positive effect on the relative wage of the workers and the indirect negative effect over their real wage due to the rise in inflation. In principle, therefore, the incentives to demand wage increases will be greater the lower the degree of centralization of wage negotiations.

Market conditions, both at the aggregate level and at the sectoral level, also affect the bargaining power of unions and firms, and hence the path of wages. In a situation of growing aggregate demand for labour, the bargaining power of unions increases, thus inducing demands for wage increases. On the other hand, the goods market poses a constraint for the individual firm which will resist increases in wage costs. The more severe the market constraint, the greater the willingness of the firm to resist wage increases, and to impose conflict costs on unions.

The goods and labour markets at the sectoral level have their own dynamics but they certainly interact. The attitude of firms in wage bargains is affected by the goods market constraint they face. Given the market constraint, the willingness of a firm or group of firms to impose conflict costs on workers grows with the demand for wage increases. If, for example, the firm chooses to peg the price to the rate of inflation in the international market, given the path of labour productivity and of non-labour costs, there is an obvious trade-off between the path of the wage and the profit margin. The actual levels of the wage and the profit margin will depend on the incentives to the union to demand wage increases (as discussed above) and the relative bargaining power of the union and the firm.

The alleviation of the goods market constraint, say by an acceleration of inflation of the relevant price in the international market, reduces the pressures over the profit margin of wage increases and, as a result, mitigates the willingness of the firm to impose conflict costs on workers. Firms become more tolerant and workers have an extra incentive to demand wage increases as market conditions become more favourable. As a result, it seems plausible to assume that both the indexation factors of wages (with respect to past inflation) and prices (with respect to costs) will tend to increase. This argument implies that, to the extent that market conditions are an important determinant of the bargaining structure between the union and the firm, the indexation factors of wages and prices will tend to move together over time.

The Structure of the Model

In this chapter we develop a model to discuss the issues raised in the previous paragraphs. Before we proceed, it seems convenient to present a brief sketch of the model and to discuss its structure. The starting point of the model is that money wages are negotiated between the union and the firms in a sector and that, given the constraints faced by the firms in the goods market and the adjustment period of wages over the year, there exists a fundamental conflict between wages and profits. The parties will try to impose costs – 'conflict costs' as we will refer to them – on each other. The size of these costs will depend on the degree of dissatisfaction of each of the parties with the distribution of the pie between them.

We will assume that the smaller the indexation parameter of prices with respect to costs – which depends on the indexation parameter of wages to CPI prices – the greater the incentives for the firms to impose conflict costs on the workers. The capacity of the union to oppose such costs will depend on the organization of the union and on the militancy of the workers. The former will be taken as an exogenous variable whereas militancy will depend on the threat of a reduction of real wages. Hence, an increase in the length of the adjustment period, for example, which implies a reduction in the real wage, leads to an increase in militancy and thus to an increase in the capacity of unions to impose costs on firms, or their capacity to respond to an attempt by the firms to impose costs on the workers. In order to increase the real wage, the union has an incentive to increase the indexation factor of wages with respect to past inflation. However, as seen in Chapter 2, the effect of an increase in the indexation factor is not independent of the size of the bargaining party or the degree of centralization of negotiations. The greater the latter, *ceteris paribus*, the greater will be the effect of an increase of money wages on inflation, and the smaller the effect on real wages.

The exercise developed below assumes that the union maximizes the difference between the gains from increasing the indexation factor of wages – taking into account the effect on future inflation – and the costs imposed by the firms as a result of the union's attempt to increase wages. The endogenous variable in the model is the optimal indexation factor of wages in a representative sector. The exogenous variables are the expected rate of inflation and the duration of the indexation period. The institutional aspects of the process of wage bargaining – in particular, the degree of centralization – and the structural factors affecting the market constraints faced by firms are also taken as part of the data.

The model is partial and incomplete in at least two different aspects. First of all, it is a partial equilibrium model in the sense that the union and the firms take as given in their decisions the expected rate of inflation (which in turn depends on their expectation on the indexation parameters of wages and prices in other sectors of the economy), the length of the adjustment period of wages and the constraints faced by the firm in the goods market.

Second, the model assumes a given level of employment in the sector in which negotiations are taking place and does not consider the effect of aggregate unemployment on the attitudes of the union or the firms. The assumption that the level of sectoral employment is constant does not necessarily imply that firms do not use the threat of unemployment as an instrument to impose costs on the union. An increase in labour turnover, for example, is not incompatible with a given level of employment and does represent a threat to the employed workers during the negotiation.

The assumption that the rate of aggregate unemployment is not relevant for the negotiating parties makes the results of the model rather restrictive since the costs of job loss for the workers depend on the tightness of the job market. This simplifying assumption is relaxed in the macroeconomic model developed in Chapter 4.

The rest of the chapter is organized as follows. First we examine the effect of changes in the indexation factor of wages on the real wage. We emphasize the effect of the degree of wage negotiation on such a relation. Then we discuss the conflict curve involving the union and the firms. The following step is to examine the decision of the union based on the costs imposed by the firms, on the one hand, and the incentives to increase the indexation factor of the wage, on the other. Finally, we discuss the effects of exogenous changes in the duration of the indexation period, the degree of centralization of wage bargains and the market constraint faced by firms.

The Wage Curve Re-stated

The wage curve describes the average real wage during the year as a function of the indexation parameter, the expected rate of inflation in the following year and the duration of the indexation period. The rate of inflation is determined by the indexation parameters of wages and prices in all sectors of the economy. Hence, in forming the expectation of the rate of inflation, the union must form a point expectation of these parameters. This is obviously a very difficult exercise especially if the degree of centralization of negotiations is low and the number of bargains scattered over the year is large. In centralized negotiations, where a few pattern setters establish an average indexation factor around which most factors will be fixed, it is much easier to form an expectation of inflation. In an environment of great volatility of the rate of inflation, the degree of uncertainty concerning the value of the indexation parameters is also very large, and the best a union can do is to make a gross estimate of the future path of prices.

In what follows we re-write equation (2.10) to emphasize the importance of looking at the expected rate of inflation as determined by the indexation parameters of wages and prices. The wage equation is given by:

$$\omega_{t,j} = \frac{\omega_{-1,j}(1 + \lambda_j v_{-1,j})}{(1 + p_{-1})[1 + p_t^e(\underline{\lambda}, \underline{\varepsilon})]^\delta} \qquad (2.10')$$

where $\underline{\lambda} = (\lambda_1, \lambda_2, ..., \lambda_n)$ and $\underline{\varepsilon} = (\varepsilon_1, \varepsilon_2, ..., \varepsilon_n)$. The vectors $\underline{\lambda}$ and $\underline{\varepsilon}$ represent the expected levels of the indexation parameters of wages and prices, respectively, in all sectors of the economy, including sector j. In making its decisions, the union must take into account not only the expectation of the values of the indexation parameters in all the other sectors but also the effect of its own indexation parameter on the rate of inflation. The greater the size of its own parameter, the greater the rate of inflation and hence, given the peak real wage, the smaller the real wage in sector j during the year.

The first relevant question for the union in deciding on the optimal value of λ_j is the following: what is the effect on the real wage of an increase in the indexation parameter? The effect can be decomposed into two parts. The first is the effect on the peak real wage and the second is the effect on the rate of inflation:

$$\frac{\Delta \omega_j}{\Delta \lambda_j} = (\frac{\Delta Peak}{Inflation}) + (\frac{Peak}{\Delta Inflation})$$

The peak real wage – that is, the wage immediately after the adjustment – is given by $\omega_{-1j} [(1 + \lambda_j v_{-1j})/(1 + p_{-1})]$ and is a positive function of λ_j. Inflation, on the other hand, is also positively affected by λ_j. Hence, the net effect of an increase in the indexation parameter on the real wage is, in principle, ambiguous. A rigorous answer to the question being asked can be given by the partial derivative of the real wage (as determined in equation (2.10')) with respect to the indexation parameter:

$$\frac{\partial \omega_j}{\partial \lambda_j} = \frac{\omega^p_{-1,j}}{(1+ p_{-1})(1+ p_t)^\delta} [v_{-1j} - \frac{\delta(1+ \lambda_j v_j)}{(1+ p_t^\epsilon)} \Theta_j(n)] > 0 \quad (3.1)$$

The crucial variable in equation (3.1) is Θ_j which we have written as a function of n, that is, the number of bargaining parties or sectors in the economy. We should recall from Chapter 2 that Θ_j measures the response of the CPI rate of inflation to a marginal change in the indexation parameter in sector j:

$$\Theta_j(n) = v_j(\frac{\partial \pi_t}{\partial \lambda_j}) \quad (2.18)$$

We should also recall that the size of Θ_j is a negative function of n, that is, the greater the number of negotiation sectors, the smaller the impact of an increase in the indexation parameters on the aggregate rate of inflation. The effect on the real wage in sector j of an increase in the indexation factor in sector j depends on the impact on the rate of inflation which in turn is a function of the size of the representative bargaining party (or the number of representative bargaining parties). If the representative sector is small, the effect on inflation – given by the value of Θ_j – will be small. As the sector becomes bigger – and the degree of centralization of wage bargaining becomes higher – the impact of an increase in λ_j on inflation will increase, and the negative effect on the real wage will become stronger.

The shape of the wage curve in the space $<\lambda_j, \omega_j>$ will be important for the ensuing analysis. In Appendix 3.1 we discuss the shape of the wage function and show under which conditions the curve is concave. In Figure 3.1 we show one straight line and two curves. Each of them correspond to a different value of Θ_j. The straight line represents the wage curve in the case in which Θ_j is zero, or the limit case in which the typical sector is so small that the impact of an increase in the indexation parameter on the rate of inflation is negligible. In such a case, the effect of an increase in λ_j on the real wage is not affected by the impact on the rate of inflation which, in fact, does not exist.

For positive values of Θ_j the wage curve has a positive slope and is concave. The positive slope results from the fact that, for relevant values of the data of the model, the effect via the increase in the peak wage dominates over the effect via the rate of inflation.[1] The latter, however, makes the curve concave. The concavity will be greater the greater the impact of an increase in λ_j on inflation, that is, the greater the value of Θ_j.

In Figure 3.1, $\Theta^1_j > \Theta^0_j$, which implies that the curve associated with Θ^1 is more concave than the curve associated with Θ^0. For a given value of λ_j, say $\underline{\lambda}_j$, the real wage will be greater for $\Theta_j = 0$ (straight line) than for $\Theta_j = \Theta^0_j$ and smaller for $\Theta_j = \Theta^1_j$. As a result, the incentives to increase λ_j will be greater the smaller the impact on the rate of inflation which, in turn, depends on the size of the typical sector or the number of sectors in the economy.

The Cost Function

Firms face a market constraint, that is, market conditions which affect the relation between the price of the goods they produce and the volume of goods they can sell. The simplest way to motivate the formalization of the market constraint is to assume that the firms in sector *j* sell their products in the international market and that the price (or price inflation) is exogenously given. Firms can not affect the international price, and, by hypothesis, if they want to keep their share of the market, their price can not increase more than the international price.[2] For the sake of simplicity we assume that this is indeed the objective of the firms, that is, to keep constant their share in the international market. Hence, given the rate of inflation in the international market (k_j), firms are supposed to equate π_j to k_j which implies that

$$\pi_{t,j} = \epsilon_f c_{t,j} = k_{t,j}$$

Given the definition of $c_{t,j}$ (see equation (2.12)), the above equation implies that:

$$\varepsilon_j = \frac{k_j}{\gamma_j(\lambda_j \nu_j - c_j) + \psi_j} \tag{3.3}$$

where $\psi_j = (1 - \gamma_j)\,\pi_t$.

Note that, given the market constraint - represented by the size of k_j - there exists a conflict between the indexation factor of the price with respect to costs (ε_j) and the indexation parameter of the wage with respect to prices (λ_j). An increase in the latter necessarily implies a reduction in the former. Such conflict is at the root of the incentives of firms to impose conflict costs on the union and vice-versa during wage negotiations. A relaxation of the market constraint – an increase in the rate of inflation of the international price – reduces the conflict and, in principle, would be compatible with a simultaneous increase of both the indexation parameters of wages and prices. Figure 3.2 shows two curves relating ε_j and λ_j. Each curve is associated with a different level of k_j: the lower the market constraint (or the greater the value of k_j), the greater the value of ε_j, given the value of λ_j, and vice-versa. Based on equation (3.3), we can establish a relation between the elasticities of the

Wage Determination in Economies with High Inflation

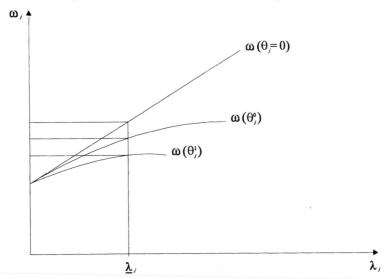

Figure 3.1 The wage curve ($\theta_j^1 > \theta_j^0$)

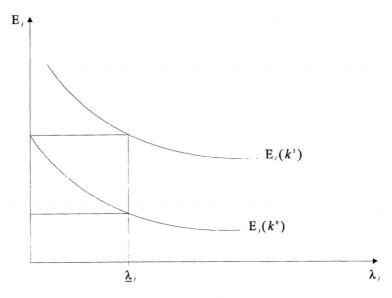

Figure 3.2 The market constraint ($k^1 > k^0$)

indexation parameters of prices and wages with respect to a change in the market constraint. Such a relation is given by:

$$\eta_{\epsilon_j, k} = 1 - z_j \eta_{\lambda_j, k} \tag{3.4}$$

where

$$z_j \equiv \frac{\gamma_j v_j \lambda_j}{\gamma_j (\lambda_j v_j - 1_j) + \Psi_j} < 1$$

The term $z_{t,j}$ is a function of the ratio between the shares of labour and non-labour costs, that is, $(1 - \gamma_j)/\gamma_j$. The smaller the share of labour costs, the smaller the size of $z_{t,j}$, and the greater the elasticity of the indexation parameter of prices compatible with a given value of the indexation parameter of wages. In the face of an increase in k_j, given the increase in wages, the increase in prices will be greater the smaller the share of wages in direct costs. Equation (3.4) will be important in the discussion of the effects of changes in market constraint below.

Equation (3.3) shows that there exists a clear friction between the interests of firms and the interests of the union bargaining in sector j. As a result of such friction, during the bargain, firms will attempt to affect the attitude of the union by imposing costs on the workers, and the union will respond by imposing costs on the firms. The typical sacrifice imposed by the union on the firms are the costs associated with the strike activity whereas the typical conflict cost imposed by the firm on the workers – besides the threat of unemployment – is the loss of wages associated with the period in which workers are on strike. The result will be a cost function representing the *net* conflict cost imposed by the firms on the workers:

$$C_j = C_j(\lambda_j, k_j, \delta) \tag{3.5}$$

where $\quad \dfrac{\partial C_j}{\partial \lambda_j} > 0, \quad \dfrac{\partial C_j}{\partial k_j} < 0, \quad \dfrac{\partial C_j}{\partial \delta} < 0$

Given the market constraint, the greater the indexation factor of wages (λ_j), the smaller will be the indexation parameter of prices (ε_j). Hence, the net cost imposed by firms on the workers will increase with λ_j ($\partial C_j / \partial \lambda_j > 0$). On the other hand, an increase in the market constraint will reduce the net costs imposed by firms on workers ($\partial C_j / \partial k_j < 0$). Finally, an increase in the length of the indexation period will reduce the real wage of workers (given the expected rate of inflation) and, as a consequence, will increase the incentives for the union to impose costs on the firms thus reducing the net costs imposed by firms on workers ($\partial C_j / \partial \delta < 0$). We will assume that C_j increases faster as the value of λ becomes greater, or that C_j is convex – that is, $\partial^2 C_j / \partial \lambda_j^2$ is positive.

In order to make the results of the exercise easier to understand, we will assume that the cost function has the following specific form:

$$C_j = \lambda_j^\beta - \mu k_j \lambda_j - \tau \delta \lambda_j \qquad (3.6)$$

where $\beta > 1$ and μ and τ are positive. Parameters β, μ and τ reflect the relative bargaining power of the union and the firms.

This cost function has the following characteristics:

$$\frac{\partial C_j}{\partial \lambda_j} = \beta \lambda_j^{\beta - 1} - \mu k_j - \tau \delta > 0$$

for $\quad \lambda_j > [\mu \dfrac{k_{j+} \tau \delta}{\beta}]^{\frac{1}{\beta - 1}}$

$$\frac{\partial^2 C_j}{\partial \lambda^2} = (\beta - 1)\beta \lambda^{\beta - 2} > 0$$

$$\frac{\partial C_j}{\partial k_j} = -\mu \lambda_j < 0$$

$$\frac{\partial C_j}{\partial \delta} = -\tau\lambda_j < 0$$

We will restrict the values of the parameters ß, μ and τ to make the function compatible with the characteristics of the general function described above.[3] Figure 3.3 depicts two costs functions each of them associated with a different value for the market constraint. The smaller the constraint (or the greater k_j) the lower the cost.

The Choice of the Optimal Indexation Factor

The union is assumed to balance between the benefits of increasing λ_j as determined by the wage function (equation (2.10)) and the costs as determined by the net cost function (equations (3.5) or (3.6)). We assume that ω_j and C_j have the same dimension, that is, that they are comparable. The principle governing the decision of the union is to maximize the difference between the benefits and the costs for the workers of increasing the indexation parameter of wages.

Accordingly, we assume that the union maximizes the following function over λ_j :

$$\Lambda_j(\lambda_j, k_j, \delta) = \omega_j(\lambda_j, \delta) - C_j(\lambda_j, k_j, \delta)$$

The first order condition for such maximization problem is given by:

$$\frac{\partial \omega_j}{\partial \lambda_j} = \frac{\partial C_j}{\partial \lambda_j} \tag{3.7}$$

or, if instead of the general equation (3.5), we take equation (3.6), the first order condition becomes:

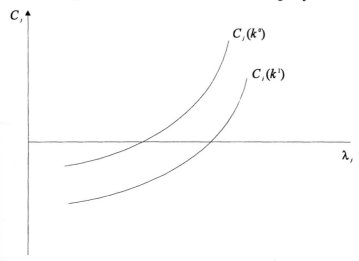

Figure 3.3 The cost function ($k^1 > k^0$)

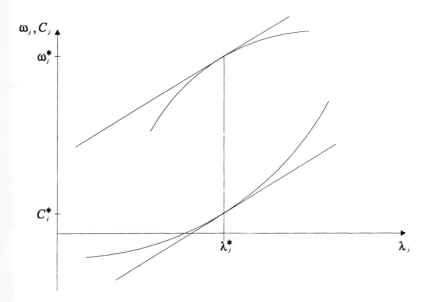

Figure 3.4 The optimal indexation factor

$$\frac{\omega^p_{-1}v_j}{(1+p_{-1})(1+p_t)^\delta} - \frac{\delta\omega^p_{-1}(1+\lambda^*_jv_j)\Theta_j}{(1+p_{-1})(1+p_t)^{1+\delta}} = \beta\lambda^{*\,(\beta-1)}_j - \eta k_j - \tau\delta$$

(3.7')

where λ^*_j is the optimal level of indexation of wages. Figure 3.4 depicts the solution of the union's maximization problem. Note that Θ_j, k_j and δ are parameters in the decision of the union: any change in these parameters will affect the optimal level of indexation. In what follows we examine the impact of changes in the parameters on the decision of the union.

The Centralization of Wage Bargains

In Chapter 2 we associated the centralization of wage bargains with the size of the parameter Θ. Before we proceed, let us reexamine this connection. We made the simplifying assumption that all sectors have the same size (that is, $\alpha_j = \alpha = 1/n$ where n is the number of sectors). Given the objectives of this study, we defined a 'sector' as a set of productive units which negotiate together with single union. Thus, a sector can either be a single plant, a single firm (with more than one plant), a restricted set of firms operating in the same industry or a more encompassing set of firms also operating in the same industry. A centralization of wage bargains, involving a greater number of firms (and unions), increases the size of the sector. In terms of our notation, a centralization of bargains increases α and reduces n.

We assume that the weight of a given sector in the formation of the aggregate price level is given by its size, that is, α_j. The greater the degree of centralization of bargains, the greater the size of the representative sector (α) and the greater the weight of the price level of goods produced in that sector in the aggregate price level. The parameter Θ_j measures the impact of an increase in the indexation parameter of wages in sector j on the CPI rate of inflation, that is, $\Theta_j = \partial p/\partial \lambda_j$. We showed in Chapter 2 that Θ_j (or simply Θ since all sectors have the same size) increases with the size of the sector or, what is the same, falls with the number of sectors. In other words, the impact of an increases in the indexation parameter of wages on inflation increase with the centralization of wage negotiations. The important point in this connection is that in a decentralized bargain, the impact of the resulting indexation parameters (of wages and prices) on the aggregate rate of inflation is negligible. In fact, the impact might be so small that the negotiating agents do not realize that an impact exists. That is, they might not be aware of the consequences for inflation of their decisions. If indeed they are not aware, their decisions will not take into account such consequences. On the other hand, if we go to the other extreme, and assume that the wage bargain is completely centralized (so that $n = 1$), the effect of the decisions of the bargaining parties on macroeconomic variables becomes very clear. As the weight of the sector on the economy increases, the impact of the decisions increases, and the consequences become more transparent. What happens in intermediate situations is not so clear. The macroeconomic impact of the decisions made during a negotiation are significant but the agents might not be aware of them.

In terms of the model presented above, the impact of changes in the degree of centralization of negotiations on the behaviour of unions can be examined through the effect of a change in Θ on the size of the optimal indexation parameter of wages. To see this, we differentiate the first order condition with respect to Θ and λ_j^*. If we take the cost function in its general specification, the result is the following:

$$\frac{\partial \lambda_j^*}{\partial \Theta_j} = \frac{-\dfrac{\partial(\partial \omega_j/\partial \lambda_j)}{\partial \Theta_j}}{\dfrac{\partial^2 \omega_j}{\partial \lambda_j^2} - \dfrac{\partial^2 C_j}{\partial \lambda_j^2}} < 0 \qquad (3.8)$$

The term in the numerator is the effect of the change in Θ on the slope of the wage function. According to equation (3.1), the effect is negative. An increase in the degree of centralization of bargains increases the impact of a change in the indexation parameter of wages on inflation. An increase in Θ reduces $\partial\omega/\partial\lambda$, that is, reduces the slope of the wage curve as a result of the stronger effect of $\Delta\lambda$ on inflation. In other words, the increase in the centralization of bargains reduces the incentives for the union to raise the indexation factor.

The first term in the denominator (from left to right) measures the concavity of the wage function, whereas the second term measures the concavity of the cost curve. The former is negative and the latter is positive.

Expression (3.8) is negative implying that an increase in the degree of centralization reduces the optimal level of the indexation parameter of wages. The result of the exercise if we consider the specific form of the cost function given by equation 3.6 is the following:

$$\frac{\partial\lambda_j^*}{\partial\Theta_j} = -\frac{\delta\omega_{-1}^p(1+\lambda_j^*v_j)}{(1+p_{-1})(1+p_j)^{1+\delta}\beta(\beta-1)\lambda_j^{*(\beta-2)}+\delta\omega_{-1}^p v_j\Theta_j} < 0 \qquad (3.9)$$

Figure 3.5 depicts the effect of an increase in Θ. The cost function is not affected by the exogenous change in Θ. The wage curve, on the other hand, becomes flatter as a result of the greater effect of changes in λ on inflation. Hence, the value of λ for which the distance between the cost and wage curves is maximum falls as shown in the figure.

The main conclusion to be drawn from this discussion is that the degree of centralization of wage bargains is not irrelevant for the behaviour of unions or to the functioning of the economy. Indeed, the centralization of wage bargains, by increasing the impact of the decisions made by negotiating parties on aggregate variables, has an effect on the actions of the agents. Not because the agents value the macroeconomic performance in itself, but because macroeconomic variables affect their own well-being. This important conclusion was put forward by economists and political scientists studying the differences in macroeconomic performance of OECD countries in the 1970s and 1980s. We will discuss the

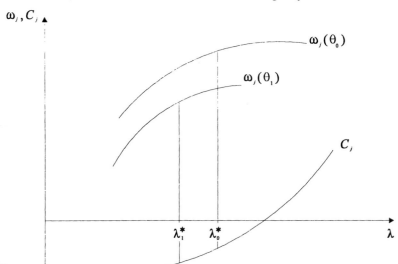

Figure 3.5 A change in the centralization of bargains $(\theta_1 > \theta_0)$

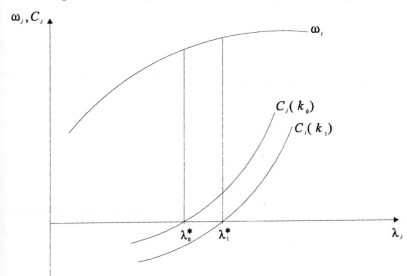

Figure 3.6 A relaxation of the market constraint $(k_1 > k_0)$

themes of the relevant literature leading to this conclusion in Chapter 5.

Changes in the Market Constraint

A relaxation of the market constraint reduces the pressures on the firms to keep inflation low. In other words, an increase in the rate of inflation of international prices, for instance, allows firms to increase the rate of inflation of their own products with a smaller risk of losing their share in the market. In principle, both the indexation factors of wages and prices could increase simultaneously. The extent to which each of them will increase depends on the bargaining power of the union and the firms which are represented by the parameters of the cost function. Using the general specification of the cost function, the effect of an increase in k_j on the indexation parameter of the wage is given by the following expression:

$$\frac{\partial \lambda_j^*}{\partial k_j} = \frac{\dfrac{\partial(\partial C_j / \partial \lambda_j)}{\partial k_j}}{\dfrac{\partial^2 \omega_j}{\partial \lambda_j^2} - \dfrac{\partial^2 C_j}{\partial \lambda_j^2}} > 0 \qquad (3.10)$$

The denominator of this expression is the same as that of equation (3.8). The numerator measures the effect of a change in k_j on the slope of the cost curve. The cost curve becomes flatter with a relaxation of the market constraint. The wage curve, on the other hand, is not affected. Equation (3.10) is positive implying an increase in the indexation factor as a result of an exogenous increase in k_j. Figure 3.6 shows the increase in the optimal indexation factor as a result of the reduction in the slope of the cost function.

The result in the case of the specific form of the cost function given by equation (3.6) is the following:

$$\frac{\partial \lambda_j^*}{\partial k_j} = \frac{\mu(1 + p_{-1})(1 + p_t)^{1 + \delta}}{\delta \omega_{-1}^p v_j \theta_j + (1 + p_{-1})(1 + p_t)^{1 + \delta} \beta(\beta - 1)\lambda_j^{* (\beta - 2)}} > 0 \qquad (3.11)$$

The effect of an increase in k_j on the indexation parameter of prices (ε_j) depends on the realtive bargaining power of the union and the firms. In principle, the effect on ε_j is unknown. We would expect the effect to be non-negative. If the market constraint becomes less severe, firms will become more lenient with the union demands, and that is why the indexation parameter of wages increase. But there are not good reasons to believe that the increase in tolerance of firms with the union will be such that the indexation parameter of prices will fall, or the profit margin will fall. They might not increase but there are not good reasons to believe that they would fall.

Formally, the effect on ε_j of an increase in k_j depends on the parameters of the cost function. According to equation (3.4), a sufficient condition for an increase in ε_j in the face of an exogenous increase in k_j is that the elasticity of λ_j with respect to k_j be smaller than 1. Such elasticity is given by:

$$\frac{\partial \lambda_j^*}{\partial k_j} \cdot \frac{k_j}{\lambda_j^*} = \frac{\mu k_j[(1 + p_{-1})(1 + p_t)^{1 + \delta}]}{\delta \omega_{-1}^p v_j \theta_j \lambda_j^* + [(1 + p_{-1})(1 + p_t)^{1 + \delta}]\beta(\beta - 1)\lambda_j^{* (\beta - 1)}} < 1$$

In Appendix 3.2 we show under which conditions $\eta_{\lambda^*,k}$ is smaller than 1 in the case of the specific form assumed by the cost function in equation (3.6). If such conditions are satisfied, what this result says is that an increase in k_j, or a relaxation of the market constraint, will lead to a simultaneous increase in both the indexation factors of wages and prices.

The results presented above are important in showing that changes in market constraints may have an effect on the path of inflation and on relative wages and prices. A reduction in tariffs, for example, or a reduction in the rate of inflation of international prices, increases the market constraint, and forces firms to reduce the rate of inflation of their prices in order to maintain competitiveness. This in turn affects their attitude towards wage negotiations and the capacity of unions to index (or overindex) wages. The degrees of indexation of wages and prices, as seen in Chapter 2, are the main determinants of the rate of inflation. Changes in market constraints which do not affect sectors uniformly will lead to changes in relative prices. The prices of goods produced in sectors where the constraint increases will tend to fall in relation to the average price level. As an extension of this effect on prices and on the attitude of firms in wage bargaining, it seems plausible to expect a reduction in relative wages in the same sectors, and hence a positive correlation between relative wages and relative prices. In other words, in sectors where the constraint increases, both firms and unions will adapt to the change, and as a result both the indexation factors of wages and prices will tend to fall.

Changes in the Length of the Indexation Period

In Chapter 2 we showed that, given the expected rate of inflation, an increase in the duration of the indexation period leads to a reduction of the average real wage, and therefore will be resisted by unions. An acceleration of inflation, on the other hand, given the length of the adjustment period, also reduces the real wage. In most Latin American countries, where the rate of inflation accelerated almost continuously during the 1980s, the period of adjustment of wages tended to fall as the rate of inflation increased. In Brazil, for example, a law established cost of living adjustments of wages every 12 months until 1979. From that year on, the adjustment period fell from one year to six months, then to three months, and in 1987 adjustments were monthly. The reduction of the indexation period is a demand of the unions in an attempt to reduce the impact of the rise in prices on the purchasing power of wages.

It can be argued that a shortening of the adjustment period fuels inflation. Indeed, if firms attempt to keep their average mark-up during the year constant, a reduction in the duration of the indexation period inevitably leads to an acceleration of inflation. It is easy to see this just by looking at equation (2.6) which relates the average real wage, the rate of inflation and the adjustment period. It is obviously very difficult to distinguish between cause and effect in this process. The acceleration of inflation induces a reduction in the indexation period through the action of the unions but, on the other hand, if firms try to keep their mark-up constant, the rate of inflation must accelerate.

In principle, from the point of view of the unions, there exists a choice between an increase in the indexation factor and a reduction in the length of the adjustment period. Either change, given the rate of inflation, is consistent with an increase in the real wage. Unions do try to negotiate the shortening of the period of indexation privately with firms, and in some cases, especially the larger firms accept a reduction even if the wage law fixes a longer period. In general, however, firms prefer to follow the law and in such cases the indexation period must be taken as a given, and the indexation factor becomes the only bargaining variable.

The effect on the attitude of unions of a shortening of the indexation period of wages is captured in the cost function through the parameter τ. *Ceteris paribus*, an increase in the indexation period (δ) reduces the real wage and makes it more vulnerable to inflationary spurs. This obviously increases the mobilization of workers around the demand to increase the indexation factor, and increases the bargaining power of the union. The assumption behind the cost function (equation (3.6)) is that the net conflict cost imposed by firms on unions falls as a result of an increase in the duration of the adjustment period.

The effect of $\Delta\delta > 0$ on the maximization problem of the union in the case where the cost function assumes the general form (equation (3.5)) is given by the following expression:

$$\frac{\partial \lambda_j^*}{\partial \delta} = \frac{\dfrac{\partial(\dfrac{\partial C_j}{\partial \lambda_j})}{\partial \delta} - \dfrac{\partial(\dfrac{\partial \omega_j}{\partial \lambda_j})}{\partial \delta}}{\dfrac{\partial^2 \omega_j}{\partial \lambda_j^2} - \dfrac{\partial^2 C_j}{\partial \lambda_j^2}} > 0 \qquad (3.13)$$

The same effect in the case of the specific cost function expressed by equation (3.6) is given by:

$$\frac{\partial \lambda_j^*}{\partial \delta} = \frac{\tau(1+ p_{-1})(1+ p_t)^{1+\delta}}{\delta\Theta_j v_j \omega_{-1}^p} - \frac{1+ p_t}{\delta\Theta_j v_j}[\ln(1+ p_t)(v_j - \frac{\delta(1+ \lambda_j v_j)\Theta_j}{1+ p_t}) + \frac{\lambda_j\Theta_j v_j}{1+ p_t}]$$

In equation (3.13) the denominator is the same as in the other two comparative statics exercises. On the numerator, the first term expresses the effect on the net cost function of an increase in δ. The effect is positive for the reasons discussed above. The second term measures the effect of an increase in δ on the impact of a change in λ on the real wage. The effect is negative: the marginal gain of an increase in the indexation factor becomes smaller as the length of the adjustment period increases. Hence the cost function and the wage function are affected by a change in δ. The slope of both fall, and for this reason the net effect on the optimal indexation factor is ambiguous.

In the second half of the 1980s, 'heterodox stabilization plans' were adopted in Argentina, Peru and Brazil. These plans were based on price and wage freezes, or price freezes coupled with an increase in the adjustment period of wages. The latter was supposed to contribute to a 'de-indexation' – or to a reduction in the degree of indexation – of the economy. That is, to reduce the dependence of today's inflation with respect to yesterday's inflation. However, it is not very clear that this is the only consequence for the inflationary process of a lengthening of the adjustment period. The uncertainty concerning the future path of inflation induced unions to demand an increase in the indexation factor as a substitute for the protection of wages against an acceleration of inflation provided by a short adjustment period. The result of course is the creation of inflationary pressures.

Conclusion

This chapter discusses some of the factors affecting the attitude of unions in bargaining wages. It argues that the extent to which wage overindexation affects inflation may be an important determinant of the behaviour of the unions. If the latter perceive the indirect effect of wage increases on the aggregate price level, the incentives to

overindex wages become smaller. Market constraints, the expected rate of inflation and the length of the indexation period are also important determinants of wages in a regime of high and chronic inflation.
It is the combination of these factors which ultimately determines the posture of workers and unions. From the point of view of the path of inflation, the most harmful scenario results from a combination of a high degree of protection against foreign competition, a low level of centralization of wage bargaining and the possibility of an inflationary shock in the future. A protected industry lets firms become tolerant and lenient in the face of wage demands. The decentralization of negotiations makes the impact of wage increases on inflation small. Finally, the prospect of an increase in inflation in the future – before the subsequent bargain – implies the possibility of a wage loss and hence increases the militancy of workers. If on top of all this we assume that the indexation period is long, so that inflationary shocks have a lasting effect on wages, the result will be a very aggressive attitude of workers and unions in wage bargains.

This was a common scenario to all the inflation-prone economies of Latin America in the 1980s. Protectionism was rooted in these economies as a result of the strategy of import substitution. The degree of centralization of bargains was very low and the possibility if inflationary shocks was always present. In Chapters 6 and 7 we will discuss in more detail the relationship between these factors and the attitude of unions in Brazil in the last decade.

Notes

1. In Appendix 3.1 we discuss the shape of the wage function.
2. Other factors such as the size of tariffs and the exchange rate would also affect the profitability of the firms and hence have an effect on the ensuing analysis.
3. The only restriction necessary is to have $\lambda_j > |(\eta k_j + \tau\delta)/\beta|^{1/(\beta-1)}$ which requires the latter expression to be small. Such condition is needed to make $\partial \tau'_j/\partial \lambda_j \cdot 0$ for the relevant values of λ_j.

Appendix 3.1 The Wage Curve

The slope and concavity of the wage function depend on the values assumed by certain variables taken as parameters in the decision of the union, namely, the rate of annual inflation (p_t), the duration of the indexation period (δ), the sum of past inflation and productivity gains in sector j $(v_{-1,j} = p_{-1} + \varsigma_{-1,t})$ and the response of inflation to changes in the indexation factor of wages in sector j (Θ_j).

The first and second partial derivatives of the wage function with respect to the indexation factor in sector j are given by the following expressions:

$$\frac{\partial \omega_j}{\partial \lambda_j} = \frac{\omega^p_{-1j}}{(1+ p_{-1})(1+p_t)^\delta}[v_{-1j} - \frac{\delta(1+ \lambda_j v_j)}{(1+ p_t^e)}\Theta_j(n)] > 0 \qquad (3.1)$$

$$\frac{\partial^2 \omega_j}{\partial^2 \lambda_j} = \frac{\omega^p_{-1j}\Theta_j}{(1+ p_{-1})(1+ p_t)^{1+\delta}}[- 2\delta v_j + \frac{(1+ \lambda_j v_j)\delta(1+ \delta)\Theta_j}{1+ p_t}] \qquad (3.2)$$

The slope of the wage function will be positive if and only if

$$\lambda_j < \frac{1+ p_t}{\delta} - \frac{\Theta_j}{v_{-1j}} \qquad (3A.1)$$

On the other hand, the wage curve will be concave if and only if

$$\lambda_j < \frac{2(1+ p_t)}{(1+ \delta)\Theta_j} - \frac{1}{v_j} - \lambda_j^{**} \qquad (3A.2)$$

These two conditions are met if we assume reasonable values for the relevant variables, including λ_j itself. For example, let us make the following assumptions:

Θ_j = 0.02

p_t = 0.30 (expected annual rate of inflation in t of 30%)

δ = 0.25 (wages adjusted every six months)

$v_{-1,j}$ = 0.25 (inflation plus productivity gains of 25% in t-1)

Given these values for the relevant variables, the first derivative of the wage function will be positive for λ_j < 5.2, whereas the function will be concave for λ_j < 100. These are very large variables for λ_j to assume. In Chapter 7, where we look at the values assumed by λ in Brazil, it will become clear that, in general, the indexation factor will assume much smaller values   seldom greater than 3.

The critical values of λ_j for the determination of the slope and of concavity of the wage function grow with inflation (p_t and $v_{-1,j}$) and the number of sectors (n) through its effect on Θ_j; and fall with the length of the adjustment period. In economies with high inflation, the annual rate of inflation is greater than 25 or 30%, the adjustment period is usually shorter than one semester and the number of sectors is very large. In general therefore, for the economies which interest us, the critical values of λ_j are greater than those shown in the example. Hence, for the relevant values of the variables, the wage curve is positively sloped and concave.

Appendix 3.2 The Correlation Between λ_j and ε_j

In the text we showed that a slackening of the market constraint will increase the optimal level of the indexation parameter of wages. That is, an increase in k_j will lead to an increase in λ_j. In principle, the effect on the indexation parameter of prices, that is, on ε_j is unknown. We would expect the effect to be non-negative. If the market constraint becomes less stringent, firms will become more tolerant with the union demands, and that is why the indexation parameter of wages increases. But there are not good reasons to believe that the increase in tolerance will be such that the indexation parameter of prices will fall, or the profit margin will fall. They might not increase but intuitively there are not good reasons to believe that they would fall.

Formally, the best way to access the effect of an increase in k_j on the indexation parameter of prices in sector j is through equation

(3.4) which relates the elasticity of λ_j and ε_j.

$$\mu_{\varepsilon_p, k} = 1 - z_j \mu_{\lambda_j, k} \qquad (3.4)$$

where $\quad z_j \equiv \dfrac{\gamma_j v_j \lambda_j}{\gamma_j (\lambda_j v_j - l_j) + \Psi_j} < 1$

Note that the smaller the share of labour costs in total direct costs (γ_j), the smaller the size of z_j on equation (3.4), and the greater the possibility of the elasticity if ε_j with respect to k_j be positive. Given the value of z_j (necessarily smaller than 1), the equation shows that a sufficient condition for $\eta_{\varepsilon,k} > 0$ is $\eta_{\lambda^*,k} < 1$. That is, the indexation factor of prices will increase with an increase in k_j only if the elasticity of the indexation parameter of wages is smaller than 1. We can show in which cases this condition is satisfied. The effect will depend on the parameters of the net cost function. If we take the specific form assumed by the cost function in equation (3.6), the elasticity of λ^* with respect to k will be given by equation (3.12):

$$\frac{\partial \lambda_j^*}{\partial k_j} \cdot \frac{k_j}{\lambda_j^*} = \frac{\mu k_j [(1 + p_{-1})(1 + p_t)^{1+\delta}]}{\delta \omega_{-1}^p v_j \theta_j \lambda_j^* + [(1 + p_{-1})(1 + p_t)^{1+\delta}] \beta(\beta - 1)\lambda_j^{*(\beta-1)}} < 1$$

$$(3.12)$$

This expression will be smaller than one if the term on the right hand side of equation (3.15) is negative:

$$(\beta - 1)\beta \lambda_j^{*(\beta-1)} - \mu k_j > - \frac{\delta \omega_{-1}^p v_j \theta_j \lambda_j^*}{(1 + p_{-1})(1 + p_t)^{1+\delta}} \qquad (3.15)$$

Hence, a sufficient condition for $\eta_{\lambda^*,k} < 1$ is that the term on the left hand side of equation (3.15) is positive. The sign of this term depends on the relation between the sizes of β and μ: if β is sufficiently large in comparison with μ, the term will be positive.

From the first order condition of the maximization problem we know that

$$\beta \lambda_j^{* \, (\beta - 1)} - \mu k_j - \tau \delta > 0$$

Hence, a sufficient condition for the left hand side of (3.15) to be positive is

$$(\beta - 2)\beta \lambda^{\beta - 1} \geq -\tau \delta$$

which is necessarily true if ß > 2 since τ and δ are positive.

In general, therefore, $\eta_{\varepsilon, k}$ will be positive if z_j is sufficiently small and ß is large in relation to μ and τ. If these conditions hold, we can say that, in the face of changes in the market constraint, the indexation factors of wages and prices will tend to move in the same direction. Alternatively, we can say that wage and price differentials should be responsive to differences in market constraints between sectors.

4. A Macroeconomic Analysis of Inflation and Stabilization

with José Márcio Camargo

Introduction[1]

The debate over stabilization programmes in Latin America could not avoid the perennial dilemma between orthodox demand management policies and incomes policies. In the early 1980s economists in the region developed a view according to which, given the pervasiveness of indexation schemes, the fight against inflation should be essentially a fight against indexation. In other words, the elimination of indexation mechanisms should be the focus of stabilization programmes.

The reasoning behind this argument had a strong Kaleckian flavour. The argument was that firms operate with a fixed mark-up and wages are indexed to past inflation. Hence the basic proposal was to freeze prices and reduce the degree of indexation of wages by lengthening the adjustment period. Demand management did not play a central role in the diagnosis of the causes of inflation. As in the most rudimentary Kaleckian or structuralist models, the mark-up was taken as given, and quite independent from the level of aggregate demand, or the level of excess demand, in the economy. Reducing aggregate demand would not have a significant effect on the determination of the mark-up or the degree of indexation of wages, and hence on inflation or the distribution of income. A more sophisticated argument was that in economies with very high inflation, demand management policies were impotent to reduce the degree of indexation of wages and prices.[2]

Another strand of thought emphasizes the role of distributive conflict in determining the path of inflation.[3] The basic view is that the economic agents – workers and firms or workers and capitalists – can not reach an agreement over the distribution of income. As a result, there is a permanent struggle between them. The size of the indexation factors of wages and prices reflect such a struggle. Workers try to recover the purchasing power of their wages since the last bargain, whereas firms try to recover the level of their mark-up after wage negotiations. This view of course has a lot in common with the fundamentals of this book.

The notion of distributive conflict is not easily tractable in a purely economic framework. Political and institutional factors play a major role in studying the concept. Chapters 5 and 6 are devoted to examining these factors. Even more difficult is to translate the theoretical notion of distributive conflict and its implications for inflationary processes into policy proposals. Policy makers and technocrats obviously can not control social forces. They may take them as given and consider them as constraints to their policy proposals. Alternatively, they can ignore them and go ahead with their policies. Of course, the latter alternative runs a serious risk of establishing policies which are incompatible with the social forces, and hence inefficient or too costly or simply not feasible. Indeed, negotiated incomes policies and 'social pacts' can be seen as institutional instruments to deal with inflation in an environment where the attitude of social actors in the face of a stabilization attempt is not insignificant.

In a sense, the 'heterodox plans' based on price and wage freezes adopted in Argentina, Brazil and Peru during the 1980s committed the sin of ignoring the notion of distributive conflict, and the political and institutional foundations of wage and price formation. The basic concern of the plans was with the elimination of indexation factors without taking into account the fact that these factors are strongly affected by the conflict between the agents in the economy over the distribution of income.

Based on some of the notions developed in Chapters 2 and 3, the present chapter is devoted to a discussion of the relationship between inflation, income distribution and the level of economic activity. We will emphasize the role of the distributive conflict between workers and firms, and will attempt to link the discussion to the roles of the level of activity and indexation in inflationary processes.

The Structure of the Model

The model developed in Chapter 2 is based on the actions of unions and firms in a partial equilibrium environment. In particular, the level of aggregate employment is taken as given and thus does not play any role in affecting the behaviour of the agents. The present model tries to overcome some of the shortcomings associated with the hypothesis of a given level of economic activity. Indeed, the level of capacity utilization is an endogenous variable of the model together with the rate of inflation and the distribution of income.

The framework of the model is quite conventional. On the one hand, using some of the elements discussed in the previous chapters, we look at the formation of wages and prices considering the roles of excess demand in the goods and labour markets. On the other hand, we have an aggregate demand function in which the distribution of income plays an important part. Thus the model follows the typical macroeconomic framework where the equilibrium is determined through the interaction of aggregate demand and supply forces.

As in most macroeconomic models, the one presented here makes the assumption that all firms behave in the same way. Put in other words, we assume that all firms and unions in the economy mimic the behaviour of a representative firm and a representative union, respectively. In the same vein, we do not consider the difference between the rates of inflation of the consumers' price index and the wholesale price index. We assume that the only relevant prices in the economy are the aggregate price level and the aggregate wage level. Furthermore, we will ignore changes in labour productivity and non-labour costs in the formation of wages and prices.

The main objective of the chapter is to integrate three factors affecting the determination of the rate of inflation and the level of activity in an economy with a chronic inflationary process: inertial factors, distributive conflict and the level of aggregate demand. We develop a model in which full indexation of wages and prices and conflict over the distribution of income between wages and profits could co-exist even in equilibrium positions.[4] However, we argue that such equilibrium is not independent from the level of aggregate demand and that, as a consequence, stabilization plans which dismiss the importance of the management of demand are, in principle, inefficient.

In order to develop this argument, the chapter is organized as follows. In the following section we establish the conditions of inflationary and distributive equilibrium. The next section is devoted to the discussion of demand equilibrium. The following task is to present the determination of macroeconomic equilibrium, that is, the simultaneous determination of the rate of inflation, the degree of capacity utilization and the distribution of income. We then examine the short-run dynamic of the model, and compare it with the dynamics of the conventional structuralist model. The final section studies the workings of demand management and incomes policies and discusses stabilization plans in regimes of high and unstable inflation. An appendix examines the stability conditions of the model.

Distributive and Inflationary Equilibrium

We start by taking Keynes' view that workers can only negotiate over money wages. The real wage and the share of wages in income depend indirectly on the economic agents' decisions at the aggregate level to allocate their wealth and spend, and directly on the pricing policy of firms. Hence, we develop a model in which unions and firms negotiate the money wage, firms determine the price level given their expectation of the level of demand for their products, and consumers and investors decide on the level of demand. The distribution of income (the share of profits) and the level of activity (the degree of capacity utilization) are endogenously determined.

In this section we develop the notions of inflationary and distributive equilibrium. When the economy is in a situation of equilibrium, both the rate of inflation and the distribution of income between wages and profits remain at stationary levels. We start by studying the formation of money wages, then the formation of prices, and finally the distribution of income.

In studying the determination of money wages in this chapter, we ignore the roles of the degree of centralization of bargains and of the length of the indexation period. These two elements ultimately determined the incentives for the union to increase the indexation factor of wages in the previous chapter. Here, we will concentrate on factors affecting the bargaining power of the union which, in Chapter 2, conditioned the capacity of firms to impose conflict costs on the workers. We assume that the union's capacity to overindex wages with respect to past inflation depends on factors affecting the degree of mobilization or militancy of workers and the following paragraphs.

Labour Mobilization and Bargaining Power

The bargaining power of unions, or their capacity to react to the conflict costs imposed by the firms, are strongly affected by the degree of mobilization of workers. In Chapter 2 we restricted the factors affecting labour mobilization to the expected real wage associated with the length of the adjustment period. Here, we will expand the list of factors.

In what follows the degree of labour mobilization will be represented by the function f (...). This function is assumed to depend on the rate of unemployment, the degree of distributive dissatisfaction of workers, and a set of institutional and political variables influenced by the stage of organization of the labour movement, the degree of political repression, and the structure of collective bargaining.

We assume that the greater the rate of open unemployment, the greater the cost for the workers of losing their jobs, and the harder it becomes for unions to organize and mobilize workers. The smaller the degree of mobilization, the smaller the power of unions to affect the rate of change of money wages.[5]

For the sake of convenience, in the model, instead of the rate of unemployment, we will use the degree of capacity utilization to represent the impact of the level of activity on the degree of mobilization of workers. The rate of capacity utilization is an imperfect substitute for the rate of unemployment. There are sectoral differences between the available supply of labour and capital. There are also differences between the aggregate supply of capital and labour. In the text we ignore these differences and assume that there is a stable relation between the rate of unemployment and the degree of utilization, and that the economy will simultaneously achieve a situation of full employment and full utilization of capacity. In short, we assume that $z = 1 - u$ where z is the degree of utilization of capacity and u the rate of unemployment.

Another element affecting labour mobilization is the degree of distributive dissatisfaction of workers, or the extent to which workers feel discontented with their real wage. The degree of dissatisfaction – which we will take as the measure of distributive conflict – is given by the difference between the target (or desired) real wage and the average wage. Alternatively, the degree of dissatisfaction can be measured by the difference between the actual share of profits and the share of profits corresponding to the target wage.[6] The greater the difference between the two, the greater the dissatisfaction and the degree of distributive conflict.

The definition of 'target wage' or 'target distributive share' is rather polemical. One possibility is to see the target wage as the average real wage in the last year. In the same vein, another alternative is to see it as a weighted average of past real wages in which recent wages have a greater weight. If the rate of inflation is stable, the two definitions will tend to coincide. Indeed, with constant inflation, according to the second definition, the target wage will converge to the current average wage just as in the first definition.[7]

Another possibility is to take the target wage as a given in the short run, that is, as a structural variable affected by long-run factors. This is the way in which we propose to treat the target wage in the following discussion. In this sense, the target wage in the model resembles the 'subsistence wage' in classical political economy.

Finally, institutional and political factors affect the degree of labour mobilization. The organization of the labour movement, the legitimacy of union leaders, the political environment, the structure of capital–labour relations and collective bargaining are all important factors affecting mobilization. In democratic capitalist economies, unemployment is usually the main weapon used by governments to reduce union activism. Alternatively, negotiations involving employers' associations, central unions and the government have been attempted in European economies to induce moderation on the part of workers. In Latin American countries, however, authoritarian regimes recurrently used political repression as a direct instrument to reduce mobilization. We will discuss the institutional and historical factors in the following two chapters. Here, they will be treated as part of the data.

To sum up the discussion on the determinants of labour mobilization, the workers' mobilization function, f (...), will be written as follows:

$$f(...) = \rho'(z-z_0) + \phi'(y-y_0) \qquad (4.1)$$

where z measures the actual degree of capacity utilization, z_0 stands for the degree of capacity utilization associated with the 'structural rate of unemployment'[8] and $(z - z_0)$ is a measure of excess demand in the labour market; and y is the actual share of profits in income, y_0 is the target share and $(y - y_0)$ is the degree of dissatisfaction or distributive gap. Both $(z - z_0)$ and $(y - y_0)$ affect labour mobilization positively: when the degree of utilization is too high compared to the structural degree, or when the profit share is too high compared with the target share, the capacity of unions to mobilize workers increases. Hence parameters ρ' and ϕ' are both positive.

The Mark-up Power of Firms

We now turn to the capacity of firms to mark-up costs or the indexation factor of prices with respect to costs as discussed in Chapter 2. It is common in the structuralist literature on inflation to assume that firms mark-up changes over direct costs in such a way that the average mark-up is virtually constant over time. Here, the actual movement of the mark-up and the share of profits in income will be treated as endogenous variables.

In Chapter 2, we argued that the indexation factor of wages and prices were affected by the market constraint where the latter was given by the rate of inflation of the price in the international market. Also, we argued that, in principle, we should expect the indexation factors of wages and prices to move in the same direction as a response to changes in market conditions.

Here, instead of taking the market constraint as given by the rate of inflation in the international market, we will treat it as a function of the level of capacity utilization. The extent to which the domestic market is protected from foreign competition and the role of the price in the international market will be treated parametrically. Accordingly, we assume that the indexation factor of prices responds positively to the rate of excess demand in the goods market. In other words, we assume that firms increase their mark-up over costs as the economy approaches a situation of planned (or full) utilization of capacity. When the economy is close to planned capacity, firms do not fear losing their market shares if they increase prices because other firms in the market will probably increase their prices as well.

In what follows, we will refer to $h(...)$ as the capacity of firms to mark up changes in costs, and will assume that it is positively affected by the difference between the actual (z) and the planned degree of capacity utilization (z_1) according to the following expression:

$$h(...) = 1 + \xi(z - z_1) \qquad (4.2)$$

with $\xi > 0$. Hence, when the economy is operating at planned capacity ($z = z_1$), firms will fully mark-up costs, that is, $h = 1$.

In accordance with our discussion in Chapter 2 on the relation between the indexation factors of wages and prices in the face of changes in market conditions, we will assume that the greater the capacity of firms to mark up costs the greater will be the capacity of unions to overindex wages.

The Money-Wage Function

We are now in a position to write the equation expressing the rate of change in money wages (w) as a function of the factors affecting the degree of mobilization or militancy of workers ($f(...)$) and the capacity of firms to mark up costs ($h(...)$). Formally, the wage equation proposed here takes the following form:

$$w = p_{t-1} + g[h(...); f(...)] \qquad (4.3)$$

where p_{t-1} is the rate of inflation in the previous year and function g expresses the 'net bargaining power' of firms and workers. Function g ultimately determines the size of the deviation of the actual change in money wages in relation to past inflation (that is, $w - p_{t-1}$). Based on our previous discussions, we should expect that $\partial g/\partial h > 0$ and $\partial g/\partial f > 0$. In words, the capacity of unions to overindex wages in relation past inflation will be greater the greater the capacity of firms to mark up costs or the greater the degree of mobilization of workers in support of the unions' demands.

In economies where the rate of inflation is chronically high, the rate of wage adjustment is usually anchored by an official rate of indexation set by a wage law. According to equation (4.3), the net bargaining power function (g) measures the effectiveness of the wage policy pursued by the government. Whenever $g > 0$, wages will grow faster than past inflation, and vice-versa.

The relation between function $g(...)$ and the indexation factor of wages (λ) defined in the previous chapters is given by the following expression:

$$g(...) = (\lambda - 1)p_{t-1}$$

Hence, overindexation is defined by the situation in which $g > 0$ or $\lambda > 1$.

Equation (4.3) can be written in linear form according to the following equation:

$$w - p_{t-1} = \alpha' + \alpha(z - z_1) + \rho(z - z_0) + \phi(y - y_0) \tag{4.4}$$

where parameter α is the linearization of the functional $g(h(...))$ and parameters w, ρ and ϕ are the linearization of the functional $g(f(...))$. Equation (4.4) says that the degree of overindexation is a positive function of the differences between the actual and planned degrees of capacity utilization ($z - z_1$), the actual and 'structural' degrees of capacity utilization ($z - z_0$) and the actual and target profit shares ($y - y_0$).

Price Formation

Turning now to the formation of prices, we assume that in fixing the rate of change of their prices, firms fully mark up past inflation (p_{t-1}). The margin of the rate of inflation in period t over inflation in $t-1$ depends on the capacity of firms to mark up the margin of wage inflation over past inflation ($w - p_{t-1}$) and on the rate of excess demand in the goods market. The latter is given by the difference at each point in time between the desired level of investment and the actual volume of saving (both as a proportion of capital) represented respectively by q^i and q^s. Formally, inflation is determined in accordance with the following equation:

$$p - p_{t-1} = h(w - p_{t-1}) + j(q^i - q^s) \tag{4.5}$$

and in linear form:

$$p-p_{t-1}=[1+\xi(z-z_1)][\alpha'+\alpha(z-z_1)+\rho(z-z_0)+\phi(y-y_0]+\chi(q^i-q^s) \quad (4.6)$$

A few observations on the inflation equation. It should be clear that z_0 and z_1 are different. The structural rate of unemployment (associated with z_0) corresponds to a level of the degree of capacity utilization which has little to do with the desired level of utilization on the part of firms. The labour market may achieve a situation of virtual full employment at 90% of capacity utilization $z_0 = 0.9$, but firms may take as a bench mark for their pricing decisions a different degree of capacity utilization, say 80% or $z_1 = 0.8$. This only implies that the level of activity affects the labour and goods markets, and the behaviour of unions and firms, differently.

A second point refers to the difference between the effect of changes in capacity utilization on the capacity of firms to mark up costs (h) and the direct effect of excess demand on inflation. The actual mark-up may increase if, even when the economy is operating at very low levels of utilization, firms increase their prices as a response to a situation of unexpected excess demand in the goods market. A sudden increase in aggregate demand independently of the degree of utilization will lead to two different effects: an adjustment through prices in the immediate run and an adjustment through output (or capacity utilization) after a while if firms expect the increase in demand to be sustained.

In simple structuralist models, it is usually assumed that as long as there is idle capacity, firms will respond to an increase in demand through changes in utilization only. Accordingly, the effect of changes in the rate of excess demand over prices (χ) is zero, and the h(...) factor is equal to 1 until the point in which the economy reaches full utilization of capacity.[9] In addition, it is assumed that money wages remain constant until the economy reaches full employment. Beyond this point inflation will accelerate because money wages will start to grow and the mark-up will increase due to the increase in h.[10]

Here we will distinguish three different effects. The effect of changes in the rate of unemployment on money wages. The effect on the firms' capacity to mark-up costs of changes in the relation between the actual and the planned degrees of utilization of capacity. And the direct effect of changes on excess demand on

67

inflation independently of the degree of utilization.[11] We will explore the difference between the three effects when we come to the discussion of short-run dynamics.

A final point refers to the different responses of oligopolist and competitive sectors to excess demand situations. In oligopolist sectors, the interdependence between the major firms in the industry leads to a response to changes in demand and costs in which the ratio of price to direct costs varies very little over the cycle. The response is well described in structuralist models in which the excess demand parameter (χ) is zero and the h factor oscillates with a small variance around 1. This only means that actual profit margins and the share of profits in these sectors are relatively stable over the cycle.

In competitive sectors, interdependence is not such an important factor, and firms will tend to increase their prices if there is excess demand (especially when the level of inventories is low) and to alter their mark-ups as a response to changes in the degree of capacity utilization. In these sectors, both the factor h and the parameter χ oscillate over the cycle, and thus do the actual mark-up

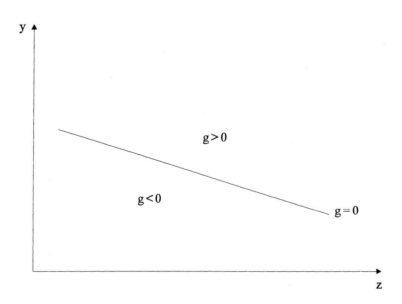

Figure 4.1 The g=0 curve

and the profit share. In short, both prices (or inflation rates) and distributive variables are more volatile in competitive sectors than in oligopolistic sectors. Given the relative levels of demand and supply, firms in the oligopolist sector can defend themselves against inflationary shocks better than those in the competitive sectors. However, in a process of expansion of demand the relative situation of competitive sectors tends to become better.

Inflationary and Distributive Equilibria

We define inflationary equilibrium as a situation in which the rate of inflation is stable. The condition for inflationary equilibrium in this model is that the net bargaining power between workers and capitalists is zero ($g = 0$) and the goods market is in equilibrium ($q^i = q^s$). In such situation $p = p_{t-1}$, and equilibrium will correspond to a situation of 'inertial inflation' in which today's inflation is equal to yesterday's inflation. When $g = 0$, the following relation between y and z holds:

$$y = \frac{\alpha z_1 + \rho z_0 + \phi y_0 - \alpha'}{\rho} - \frac{(\alpha + \phi)}{\rho}z \qquad (4.7)$$

which implies that the slope of the $g = 0$ curve is given by the expression:

$$\frac{\partial y}{\partial z}\Big|_{g=0} = -\frac{(\alpha + \rho)}{\phi} \qquad (4.8)$$

In Figure 4.1 we depict the $g = 0$ curve. Notice that above the curve, for a given profit share, the degree of utilization is greater than the one corresponding to $g = 0$, implying a positive net bargaining power of workers, and vice-versa for points below the curve. Whenever the net bargaining power of workers is positive, wages will overindex past inflation thus creating inflationary pressures.

The paths of the actual mark-up (σ) and the share of profits in income (y) are given by the following expression. A double-underlined variable indicates its absolute rate of change over time, that is, for variable x, $\underline{x} = dx/dt$:

$$\underline{y} = (1-y)\underline{g} = (1-y)(p-w)$$

$$= (1-y)[\xi(z-z_1)[\alpha'+\alpha(z-z_1)+\rho(z-z_0)+\phi(y-y_0)]+\chi(q^i-q^s)] \quad (4.9)$$

Distributive equilibrium is defined as a situation in which the distributive variables assume a stable value, that is, in which $\underline{y} = \underline{g} = 0$. The locus of points on the space $<z, y>$ for which the equilibrium condition is satisfied is given by the following expression:

$$\underline{y} = 0 \Rightarrow \frac{\partial y}{\partial z}\bigg|_{\underline{y}=0} = -\frac{\xi g + \xi(z-z_1)(\alpha+\rho)+\chi(q^i_z-q^s_z)}{\xi(z-z_1)+\chi(q^i_y-q^s_y)} \quad (4.10)$$

The slope of the $\underline{y} = 0$ curve can be either positive or negative depending on the values of g and of the relative responses of saving and investment to changes in capacity utilization and the distribution of income.

Looking at equation (4.9), it becomes clear that the path of the share of profits in income depends on the value of the net bargaining power (g) and the excess demand situation in the goods market. In particular, $g = 0$ and $q^i = q^s$ imply a situation of distributive equilibrium. Hence, the conditions for inflationary equilibrium and distributive equilibrium are exactly the same, and as a consequence, on the space $<z, y>$, the $g = 0$, $q^i = q^s$ and $\underline{y}$ curves intercept in the same point.

Aggregate Demand Equilibrium

The equilibrium between income and expenditure, or aggregate demand equilibrium, corresponds to a situation in which saving equals investment. Assuming that the propensity to save out of wages is zero, and out of profits is s, saving as a proportion of the stock of capital can be written as follows:

70

$$q^s = \frac{S}{K} = \frac{s}{Q} \frac{Q}{X'} \frac{X'}{K} = syz \qquad (4.11)$$

where K is the stock capital, Q is the volume of profits and X' is the level of potential output or the level of output associated with the full utilization of capacity. Thus, saving as a proportion of capital depends on the propensity to save out of profits (s), the share of profits in output (y) and the degree of capacity utilization (z). The rate of profit (r) is given by the ratio of total profits (Q) to the stock of capital (K). Hence, $(Q/X')(X'/K) = Q/K = r = yz$. This expression implies that equation (4.11) can be written as a function of the rate of profit as in the following expression:

$$q^s = sr$$

which of course is the classic 'Cambridge equation'.

As for the investment function, we assume that firms will consider two factors in their decision to invest. First, they will invest more the greater the expected profit per unit of output (or the expected profit margin) and, given the labour output ratio, the greater the share of profits in output. But not only the profitability per unit of output matters for the decision to invest. For a given profit margin, firms will invest more, the greater the expected degree of capacity utilization. As noted above, it is the combination of these two factors – the profit margin and the utilization of capacity – which determines the rate of profit, the ultimate determinant of investment.[12] Hence the investment: capital ratio can be written as follows:

$$q^i = \frac{I}{q} = q^i(z,y) \qquad (4.12)$$

with $q^i_z > 0$, $q^i_y > 0$

Demand equilibrium requires the equalization of the q^i and q^s ratios. A family of demand equilibrium curves can be depicted on the $< z, y >$ space. The position of the curves will depend on the propensity to save out of profits and the exogenous components of aggregate demand such as the government deficit. The slope of the equilibrium demand curve – referred to in what follows the IS curve – is given by:

$$\frac{\partial y}{\partial z}\Big|_{IS} = -\frac{q_z^i - sy}{q_y^i - sz} \qquad (4.13)$$

In principle, the slope of this curve can be positive or negative. The conventional stability condition according to which saving is more sensitive than investment to changes in the level of activity or the utilization of capacity,[13] implies that $sy > q_z^i$, that is, a negative numerator. On the denominator, saving can be more or less sensitive than investment to changes in the share of profits. If investment responds strongly to changes in the share of profits, and the denominator in equation (4.13) is positive, the slope of the equilibrium demand curve will be positive, and an increase in the profit share will be associated with an increase in the degree of capacity utilization. Marglin and Bhaduri (1990) refer to this case as the 'exhilarationist case'. If the effect of a change in the distribution of income over consumption is stronger than the effect over investment, the IS curve will have a negative slope. This is referred to as the 'stagnationist case'. In the ensuing analysis we will concentrate on the latter case.

In Figure 4.2 we depict the demand equilibrium curve corresponding to the stagnationist case. Points below the equilibrium curve are associated with a situation in which the share of profits is smaller than the equilibrium share, and therefore investment exceeds saving, characterizing a situation of excess demand in the goods market. Points above the curve are associated with situations of excess supply.

In order to have a dynamic equation for the degree of capacity utilization, we must consider the following relationship between the rate of capacity utilization (z), the level of output (X) and the level of potential output (X'):

72

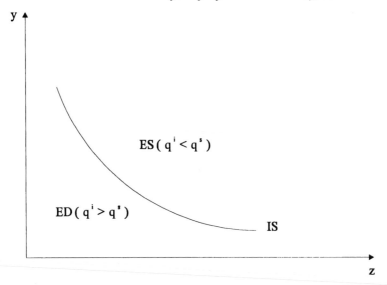

Figure 4.2 Aggregate demand equilibrium (stagnationist case)

$$X = zX'$$

which implies the following relation between their proportional rates of change:

$$\frac{\dot{z}}{z} = \frac{\dot{X}}{X} - \frac{\dot{X'}}{\underline{X}}$$

Since we shall focus the analysis on the short run, we can safely ignore changes in the stock of capital and assume $\dot{\underline{X}} = 0$. We will postulate that changes in output (and given our assumption, capacity utilization) are proportional to the difference between the desired investment and saving ratios:

$$\dot{z} = \theta[q^i(y,z) - sz]z, \quad \theta > 0 \qquad (4.14)$$

This equation implies that capacity utilization will be in a position

73

of rest only when the system is on the IS curve, that is, when the system is in a situation of demand equilibrium.

Macroeconomic Equilibrium

We are now in a position to study the characteristics of the equilibrium configuration. Macroeconomic equilibrium is defined as the situation in which the goods market is in equilibrium (IS) and the bargaining power of workers is null ($g = 0$). Together these two conditions imply a situation of simultaneous inflationary and distributive equilibria. Given the datum of the system (propensity to save, animal spirits, government deficit and determinants of the shape of functions $f(...)$ and $h(...)$), the equilibrium levels of the capacity of firms to mark up costs h^*, the degree of labour mobilization f^*, the share of profits y^*, and the degree of capacity utilization z^* are simultaneously determined. When the system deviates from the equilibrium, the share of profits and the degree of capacity utilization adjust simultaneously.

Figure 4.3 depicts the equilibrium position for $z < z_1$ in which case the $y = 0$ curve is negatively sloped. In a situation of excess demand in the goods market (that is of points to the left of the IS curve), the term $\chi(q^i - q^s)$ gives rise to forces which increase the share of profits. If $z < z_1$ (that is, if the capacity to mark-up $h(...)$ is smaller than 1), money wages must be growing in relation to past inflation to balance the direct effect of excess demand on prices, and make $y = 0$. In other words, the net bargaining power $g(...)$ must be positive. On the other hand, when there is excess supply, wages must be falling in relation to past inflation to make $y = 0$, implying a negative value of $g(...)$. Hence, for $z < z_1$, the $y = 0$ curve necessarily slopes downwards.[14]

It is important to note that the IS, $g = 0$ and $y = 0$ curves intercept on the same point. This is so because the combination of the conditions behind the IS and $g = 0$ curves lead to a situation of distributive equilibrium. Thus, in the equilibrium position the rate of inflation and the distribution of income are in a stationary position and aggregate supply equals aggregate demand.

It is interesting to note that the equilibrium configuration does not necessarily imply the absence of conflict as defined by a discrepancy between the workers' target profit share and the actual

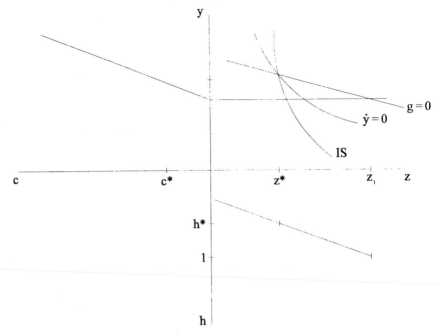

Figure 4.3 Macroeconomic equilibrium

profit share. Indeed, the equilibrium share of profits may be greater than the target share, implying the existence of dissatisfaction on the part of workers and distributive conflict. In Figure 4.3, the equilibrium share y^* is greater than the target share y_0. The curve on the first quadrant corresponds to the level of conflict as measured by $(y - y_0)$. The greater the equilibrium share, the greater the degree of conflict.

However, if the system is in equilibrium, the conflict is only latent and does not manifest itself through the effect of the bargaining power of workers on the rate of inflation. That is, at the equilibrium degree of utilization (and corresponding rate of unemployment), unions are unable to translate workers' dissatisfaction with the distribution of income into changes of money wages in relation to past inflation. In terms of the language of Chapter 2, the indexation factor of wages is equal to 1 implying that wage inflation will be equal to the rate of price inflation in the previous period.

Also, it should be noted that the equilibrium degree of capacity utilization may be either greater or smaller than the degree which makes the capacity of firms to mark up costs (h) equal to 1. The equilibrium level of h depends on the relation between the equilibrium level of capacity utilization (z^*) and the planned level of utilization (z_1). In Figure 4.3 the third quadrant depicts the h line. For values of z smaller than z, the capacity to mark up will be smaller than 1, and vice-versa.

Short-Run Dynamics

The short-run dynamics of this model depends crucially on the response of money wages to the difference between the actual and the structural rates of unemployment ($z - z_0$), the response of the capacity to mark up to differences between the actual and full (or planned) capacity utilization ($z - z_0$), and the direct response of inflation to excess demand ($q^i - q^r$).

In order to highlight the features of the model, we may compare it with a stylized structuralist model. In the latter, it is assumed that the economy is always very far from the levels of 'full employment' and 'full utilization of capacity'. In practice, it is assumed that money wages do not depend on the rate of unemployment and the capacity to mark up (h) is equal to 1 independently of the level of activity. In the model, these assumptions imply that the parameters measuring the impact of z = z_1 on prices and the impact of $z - z_0$ on wages are null, or that α = $\rho = 0$, respectively. Also, the direct effect of excess demand on inflation is neglected implying that χ = 0.[15] Indeed, in structuralist-type models, only capacity utilization responds to excess demand. Given these assumptions, the rate of change of wages and prices are given by :[16]

$$w = p = p_{t-1} + \alpha' + \phi(y - y_0) \qquad (4.15)$$

Note that, given these assumptions, only one level of the share of profits – call it y^{**} – will be consistent with a situation of inflationary and distributive equilibrium, namely,

For any share of profits greater than y^{**}, inflation will accelerate without limit. Hence, in this stylized structuralist model with full

$$y^{**} = y_0 - (\frac{\alpha'}{\phi})$$

indexation, the existence of conflict is inconsistent with a stable rate of inflation. Only if indexation was incomplete, that is, if

$$p = \frac{\alpha + \phi(y - y_t)}{1 - v} \tag{4.16}$$

wages and prices were indexed to vp_{t-1}, with $v < 1$, instead of p_{t-1}, would the system converge to a situation of stable inflation *cum* conflict. In such a case, if capitalists were able to impose a profit share greater than y^{**}, say y', the equilibrium rate of inflation would be given by:
Note that the greater the indexation factor v, the greater the equilibrium rate of inflation. In the limit, when $v = 1$, the rate of inflation will tend to explode if $y > y_0 - (\alpha'/\phi)$. Hence, in this model, full indexation and conflict cannot co-exist in equilibrium.

In Figure 4.4, we depict the structuralist case. The level of prices will be stable only if y^*, that is, the share of profits, should be smaller than the target share to compensate for the effect of α' on inflation. Inflation will be greater the greater the degree of indexation, that is, the greater v.

An intermediate model between the structuralist model and the model presented in this chapter would still ignore the response of money wages to changes in the rate of unemployment, and the response of the capacity to mark up to changes in capacity utilization. It would consider, however, the direct effect of excess demand in the goods market on the rate of inflation $\chi > 0$.[17] In such a model, not only capacity utilization but also the rate of inflation, and hence the actual mark-up and the distribution of income, would respond to changes in excess demand in the goods market.

Our model adds to the one just mentioned the effect of changes in the level of activity (or capacity utilization) on money wages and the capacity of firms to mark up. Here, both distributive conflict and the rate of unemployment affect labour mobilization. The actual mark-up, in turn, depends on the relation between the current degree

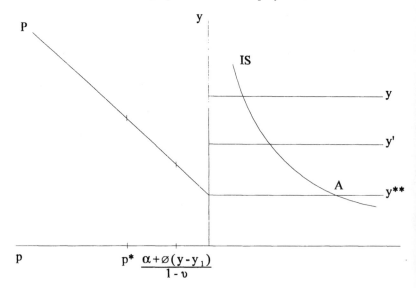

Figure 4.4 The stylized Kaleckian model

of utilization and the planned degree, and the size of excess demand (or supply) in the goods market. In Figure 4.5 we depict the stable equilibrium case.[18] The dynamics of z is given by the situation of excess demand or excess supply in the goods market. In regions A and D, the profit share is too high compared to the share corresponding to the aggregate demand equilibrium curve (IS), and since the response of consumption to changes in the distribution of income is stronger than the response of investment in the stagnationist case, there is a tendency for capacity utilization to fall. The opposite is true in regions B and C.

The dynamics of y is determined by the combination of the situation of excess demand or supply in the goods market and the size of the capacity of firms to mark up costs (h) and of the bargaining power of workers (g). In regions A and B, the share of profits is too high compared to the distributive equilibrium curve. Region A corresponds to situations of excess supply which tend to reduce the profit margin and profit share[19]. On the other hand, if the capacity to mark up costs (h) is sufficiently small, the effect of the

78

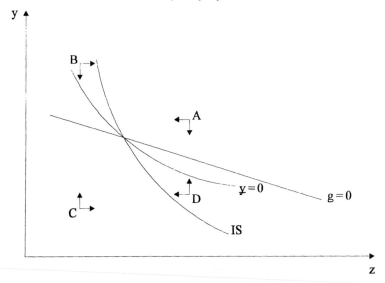

Figure 4.5 The complete model

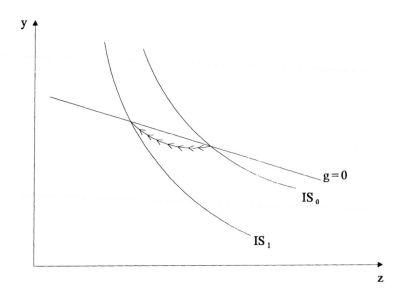

Figure 4.6a Restrictive demand policy

positive distributive conflict factor (implying a positive value for *g*) also leads to a fall in the profit share simply because the increase in money wages is not being completely marked up.[20] Similar reasoning applies to the other regions. As noted already, in this model, the presence of a conflict gap is not inconsistent with a situation of full indexation and inertial inflationary equilibrium. Contrary to the stylized structuralist model, in which money wages are driven by the conflict gap only, here distributive and inflationary equilibrium result from a balance between two forces affecting the bargaining power of unions: the conflict gap and the excess demand situation in the labour market. Hence, assuming complete indexation of wages and prices, depending on the rate of unemployment, any level of the profit share could be consistent with a position of inflationary equilibrium.

The policy implications of this result are quite important. In a structuralist model, as long as there is distributive equilibrium, that is, as long as $y = y^{**}$, changes in the determinants of aggregate demand will only affect the utilization of capacity. In the complete model presented here, changes in aggregate demand affect the bargaining balance, and hence the rate of inflation and the distribution of income. Thus, a policy implication of the structuralist model is that demand does not matter, while in the model discussed here, demand may play a pivotal role in stabilization policies.

In the structuralist model, if the economy is in a situation of distributive equilibrium and pure inertial inflation ($p_t = p_{t-1}$), the elimination of the indexation factor and a price freeze will be sufficient to stop inflation, independently of what happens to the level of aggregate demand. According to our model, the initial situation of equilibrium is only consistent with one level of aggregate demand and capacity utilization. Hence a minor change in demand will be sufficient to throw the economy in a path which is inconsistent with the price freeze.

Stabilization Policies

Three types of stabilization policies can be studied with the aid of this model: orthodox demand contraction policies, incomes policies, and heterodox shocks. In Figure 4.6a we consider the effect of a shift to the left of the IS curve due to a reduction in the fiscal deficit. A situation of excess supply will be the first effect leading to a reduction in the rate of inflation and the share of profits. In the second phase, capacity utilization will start falling. The reduction in utilization (and employment) will reduce labour mobilization and the capacity of firms to mark-up costs. However, if $z < z_1$, h will be smaller than 1 implying that price inflation will fall less than wage inflation, thus leading to an increase in the profit share. Hence, in this example, demand contraction would tend to reduce the rates of inflation, capacity utilization and employment, and increase the profit margin and share.

An alternative stabilization programme would be an incomes policy. In an authoritarian political regime one possible alternative is to repress labour activities and reduce the capacity of unions to mobilize labour. This will reduce the value of $g(...)$ or the values of parameters ρ and ϕ, and thus shift the $g = 0$ curve to the right as in Figure 4.6b. If h is smaller than one, wage inflation falls more than price inflation leading to an increase in the share of profits. The increase in the share of profits will lead to a reduction in capacity utilization, and thus a reduction in wage and price inflation. The end result will be the same as in the case of a restrictive demand policy.

From the above discussion it becomes clear that it would be rather difficult to implement a negotiated incomes policy in an economy with stagnationist features. Unions would not be content with a plan in which both the real wage and the rate of employment would fall. In an exhilarationist-type economy, in which the IS curve would be positively sloped, the real wage and the share of wages in income would still fall with a negotiated reduction in labour militancy (a reduction in g) but there would be an increase in both capacity utilization and employment. Thus it seems that a successful negotiated incomes policy would require either a strong response of investment to changes in profitability or an active demand policy on the part of the government to balance the effect of the reduction in the wage share on aggregate demand. In figure 4.6b, a shift in the IS curve to the right could combine a reduction in inflation with an increase in utilization and employment.

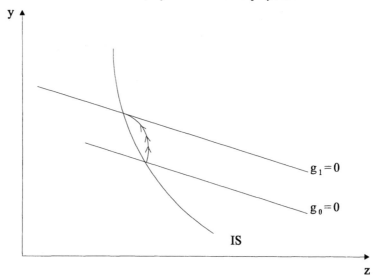

Figure 4.6b Incomes policy

Conclusion: Stabilization Policies in Regimes of High Inflation

In very simple terms, the problem with stabilization policies in regimes of high (and unstable) inflation is to bring the system back to a 'stable region'. Based on the analysis developed in this chapter, it seems clear that this might require a combination of incomes policy and demand management policy. This combination, in turn, may require institutions which make the incomes policy effective and the hardship of demand control acceptable to the major social actors in society.

A heterodox shock is a type of incomes policy. The two basic presumptions of the inertialist thesis – on which heterodox policies were adopted in some Latin American countries in the 1980s – are that, first, the economy is in a situation of distributive and inflationary equilibrium, that is a situation of purely inertial inflation, and that, second, neither the $g = 0$ nor the demand equilibrium curves will suffer any significant change after the shock. If these are the actual and relevant conditions, inflation is indeed purely neutral in terms of the distribution of income and the level of activity, and could be eliminated with the abolition of the indexation factor and a wage and price control.

An important issue in the discussion of heterodox programmes is the initial situation of the economy. If the stabilization plan is preceded by a period of high and accelerating inflation, there is a probability that the economy will not be in a position of distributive or inflationary equilibrium. If this is the case, it becomes difficult to control prices and wages. The fact that the economy is not in a position of distributive equilibrium means that the prevailing combination of real wages and degree of utilization of capacity is inconsistent with a price and wage freeze.

Like any income policy, the success of heterodox shocks depends on a certain degree of implicit acquiescence of the major social actors, or the explicit negotiation between them. The greater the degree of acquiescence, the greater the credibility of the government implementing the plan. A negotiation is not always feasible. We will argue in the following chapter that an adequate institutional structure is a prerequisite for the success of a negotiated incomes policy a structure in which the major social groups are centrally organized and the process of collective bargaining is relatively centralized. A centralized system guarantees that all the major groups are represented in the process of negotiations which, in turn, implies that these groups will feel responsible for the implementation of the programme, and will prevent the operation of free riders. The degree of synchronization of wage adjustments, on the other hand, facilitates the observance by workers of 'fair relativities' which could benefit other groups to the exclusion of the group concerned. This is true,especially in periods of high and unstable inflation in which unions and firms try to defend themselves from the uncertainties of future inflation.

In the absence of these institutions it is very difficult to implement a successful incomes policy. In Brazil these institutions did not exist when the heterodox shocks were applied. After 20 years of military regime, the labour movement was very disorganized and fragmented. There were also political reasons for the absence of negotiations. Entrepreneurs did not really think of unions as legitimate actor at the national level. The degree of credibility of the government was quite low which prevented it from calling a negotiation. On the other hand, after years of falling wages, wages were starting to recover, and unions were not very sensitive to an appeal to negotiate.

In Israel a similar programme was adopted in 1985. However, after the price freeze was announced, a wage agreement was signed between the Histadrut (the strong trade union federation) and employers. This negotiation made unions and entrepreneurs responsible for the success of the plan. This obviously reduced the chances of a major group feeling excluded from the programme. A third factor affecting the performance of heterodox shocks is the behaviour of demand. In general, a restrictive demand policy could affect the dynamic of the system after the shock, increasing the chances of a soft landing. A certain degree of demand restriction prevents the appearance of inflationary pressures. The importance of demand policies is greater in the case of a non-negotiated programme than in the case of a negotiated programme or in the case in which the distributive equilibrium before the plan was achieved. In the latter two cases the distributive problem is, so to speak, resolved, that is the size of the net bargaining power factor (factor *g*) is zero or close to zero.

Notes

1. This paper was originally prepared for the WIDER Macroeconomic Policy Project coordinated by Stephen Marglin, and was written together with José Márcio Camargo. We are grateful to Tariq Banuri, Alain Lipietz, Jaime Ros, Juliet Schor and Jose Carlos dos Reis Carvalho for their comments. Stephen Marglin, Lance Taylor and Marcello Estevão provided decisive suggestions for the development of the model.
2. See Modiano (1985a, 1985b) and Lopes (1984).
3. See Rowthorn (1981).
4. Equilibrium positions are characterized by a stable rate of inflation, degree of capacity utilization and distribution of income between wages and profits.
5. The extent to which the rate of open unemployment is a good measure of unions' capacity to mobilize workers depends on the degree of segmentation in the labour market. In the case of a low degree of segmentation, unemployed workers in the formal sector can replace employed workers in the informal sector. Hence the rate of employment (rather than unemployment) in the formal sector becomes the right variable to look at in this case. If, however, the market is highly segmented, workers from one segment cannot or do not move from one segment to the other, and therefore the rate of open unemployment becomes a reasonable measure of the potential influence of the power of unions to affect the money wage.
6. If the productivity of labour is fixed (as we shall assume), there is a linear and inverse relationship between the real wage and the share of profits in income $y = (1 - \omega b)$ where y is the share of profits ω the real wage and b the labour output relation.
7. See Ros (1988) for a detailed discussion of this point.
8. The structural rate of unemployment is associated with all forms of voluntary unemployment (such as search) as well as discrepancies between the size and composition of capital and the size and abilities of the available labour force.

9. The great majority of structuralist models of inflation make these assumptions. Indeed, they constitute a basic ingredient of the models used in the formulation of the heterodox shocks. An exception to this rule is Taylor (1985) who makes changes in money wages a function of excess demand in the labour market and changes in prices a function of both changes in costs (money wages) and excess demand in the goods market.

10. See Rowthorn (1981) for a dichotomy of models in which the distinguishing element is the size of h depending on the degree of capacity utilization. For $z < z_1$ all the adjustment goes through changes in utilization, n remains fixed and equal to 1, and prices remain constant. When z reaches z_1, that is, capacity becomes 'fully' utilized, only the mark up and therefore prices adjust to changes in demand. In Marglin (1984) $z = z_1$ ex-hypothesis, and the combination of excess demand and distributive conflict give rise to an inflationary process. Dutt's (1987) inflation model assumes that both workers and capitalists have a target distribution of income, and that the level of activity does not affect either money wages or the profit margin. In a sense, it is a pure model of distributive conflict.

11. We are grateful to Stephen Marglin for pointing out the importance of this distinction.

12. For a discussion of alternative formulations of the investment function see Steindl (1952), Rowthorn (1981), Taylor (1983, 1991), Dutt (1984, 1987), Marglin (1984), Marglin and Bhaduri (1986, 1990) and Amadeo (1986).

13. Marglin and Bhaduri (1990) refer to this condition as the Keynesian condition.

14. Following the same reasoning, it can be shown that when $z > z_1$, the $\underline{y} = 0$ curve slopes upwards.

15. This seems to be an appropriate model for describing the oligopolist sector when the economy is operating with ideal capacity and unemployed workers. But clearly it is not an adequate model to describe an economy with a reasonably large competitive sector and chronic inflation.

16. Here is the interpretation of α' in the price equation: it reflects the ability of firms to completely mark up costs, and as a result, the ability of workers to increase wages by α'. It could be assumed that $\alpha' = o$, in which case the price equation would be given by: $p = \phi (y - y_0)$ and $p = 0$ when $y = y_0$.

17. Formally, the model would be described by the following equations: $w = p_{-1} + \phi (y_0 - y)$; $p = p_{-1} + \phi (y_0 - y) + \chi [q^i(y,z) - syz]$; $\underline{y} = (1-y)(\chi [q^i(y,z) - syz]$ the $\underline{y} = 0$ curve would have its slope given by: $\partial y / \partial z \mid_{y=0} - (q^i_z - sy) / (q^i_y - sz) = \partial y / \partial z \mid_{i=r}$.

18. We study the stability conditions for both the stagnationist and exhilarationist models in the appendix.

19. This effect comes from the excess demand factor in the price equation.

20. If the capacity to mark up were greater than 1, the effect on the actual mark-up would be positive. The net effect over the mark up would depend on the relative size of the direct excess demand effect on prices and the indirect effect through the increase in wages and the capacity to mark up.

Appendix 4.1 Stability Conditions

In this appendix we study the stability conditions of the complete model. the two dynamic equations describe, respectively, the path of the share of profits in income and the path of the utilization of capacity:

$$H(y,z) = \underline{y} = (1-y)[\xi(z-z_1)[\alpha'+\alpha(z-z_1)+\rho(z-z_0+\phi(y-y_0+$$

$$+\chi(q^i(y,z)-syz)]$$

$$G(y,z) = \underline{zz} = \theta[q^i(y,z)-syz]z$$

The Jacobian is given by the partial derivatives of H and G with respect to y and z:

$$J = \begin{bmatrix} G_z & G_y \\ H_z & H_y \end{bmatrix}$$

where, observing that we are analysing equilibrium points:

$$G_z = \theta(q_z^i-sy)z$$

$$G_y = \theta(q_y^i-sz)z$$

$$H_z = (1-y)[(\alpha+\rho)\xi(z-z_1)+\chi(q_z^i-sy)]$$

$$H_y = (1-y)[\xi\phi(z-z_1)+\chi(q_y^i-sz)]$$

The trace of the Jacobian is given by:

$$T = \theta(q_z^i-sy)z+(1-y)[\xi\phi(z-z_1)+\chi(q_y^i-sz)]$$

and the determinant by:

$$\Delta = [\phi(q_z^i - sy) - (\alpha + \rho)(q_y^i - sz)]\theta z(1 - y)\xi(z - z_1)$$

A summary of the sufficient stability conditions are given in the table below:

Stability Conditions

Model	Case	Condition
Exhilarationist	stable	$z < z'$
	unstable	$z' < z < z$
	saddle	$z > z_1$

Model	Case	Condition
Stagnationist	stable	$z < z_1$ and $\partial y/\partial z\big|_{is} < \partial y/\partial z\big|_{g=0}$
	stable	$z_1 < z < z'$ and $\partial y/\partial z\big|_{is} > \partial y/\partial z\big|_{g=0}$
	saddle	$z > z_1$ and $\partial y/\partial z\big|_{is} < \partial y/\partial z\big|_{g=0}$
	unstable	$z > z'$ and $\partial y/\partial z\big|_{is} > \partial y/\partial z\big|_{g=0}$

where $z' = z_1 - \dfrac{\chi}{\phi\xi}(q_y^i - sz)$

5. Unions' Attitudes, Social Structures and Wage Restraint

Introduction

Since the mid-1970s increasing attention has been dedicated to the institutional and structural factors affecting the determination of money wages in both the political science and economics literatures. By the late 1960s, the 'golden age of capitalism', characterized by high levels of investment, growing productivity and consumption per capita, and stable prices and distributive shares in the advanced OECD economies, seemed clearly over.[1] The slowdown of productivity and the oil shocks of 1974 and 1979 made the trade-off between inflation and unemployment – the Phillips curve – more stringent.

During the 1970s and 1980s, there was a marked deterioration in the performance of all economies, albeit with some diversity in national experiences.[2] Wage restraint has been seen as a major ingredient in explaining the relative success of certain economies in coping with the crisis.[3] In countries in which the unions' attitudes are conducive to wage restraint, the macroeconomic performance (as measured by some combination of inflation and unemployment) has been clearly superior to the performance of those in which union militancy and wage demands have not diminished.

The notion that labour market institutions matter in shaping macroeconomic outcomes has become quite widespread. The huge literature on unions' and employers' associations, patterns of wage bargaining, concerted incomes policies, neo-corporatism and pluralism, and macroeconomic performance has been able to divert (at least some) economists from simplistic, institutional-free approaches to the problems of unemployment and stabilization. Orthodox economists have learned from and indeed contributed to this literature and, in a sense, have created the possibility for a Keynesian comeback.[4]

The aim of this chapter is to provide an overview of this literature in order to discuss the relation between institutional aspects of wage bargaining and stabilization policies. The chapter starts with a discussion of the logic of unions' attitudes in wage bargaining in an attempt to highlight the costs and benefits associated with wage restraint. This discussion makes the bridge between the formal models presented in Chapters 2 to 4 and the institutional analysis of the present chapter. Using examples from advanced OECD countries, the next step is to relate the conditions of wage restraint to the literature on union movement centralization, trade dependency, workers' militancy, neo-corporatism, and stabilization policies. We then create a taxonomy of industrial relations systems, and identify two 'ideal cases' – the corporatist and pluralist cases – and two 'hybrid' cases. We conclude that certain hybrid characteristics are not conducive to wage moderation and have a potential to generate unstable macroeconomic outcomes, and to render particular economic policies either infeasible or ineffective.

Structural and Institutional Determinants of Wage Restraint

In principle, unions act in the name of their members and have to confront employers on the bargaining table. In addition, they have to take into account the economic policies of the government in making their demands and, in certain cases, the orientation of confederations and political parties. Union leaders have to ponder over the objectives and interest conflicts of these different groups in making their decisions concerning wage demands. They also have to take into account their own interests as a group which implies preserving their legitimacy by being loyal to the members and keeping their credibility with the opposing negotiating parties. In the following section we look at the logic of unions' attitudes in wage bargaining, and try to picture union leaders as pivotal agents in this network of interest accommodation.

The Logic of Unions' Attitudes in Wage Bargaining

We may take as a starting point the objective of a union when negotiating the determination of money wages (w). Depending on the circumstances, unions will have different objective functions. In economies in which the monetary and fiscal policies are accommodative, that is in which the government and central bank recurrently accommodate inflationary pressures with the aim of keeping low rates of unemployment, unions may well concentrate on maximizing the real wage of their members. However, in general, we may assume that some degree of trade-off exists between the real wage and the level of employment in which case unions will look at the wage bill rather than the real wage as their target variable. Accordingly, we assume that unions try to maximize the real income of their members as represented by ωL where ω is the real wage and L is the level of employment. In maximizing its members' income, the union faces a variety of uncertainties and constraints:

[a] Two elements which the union might take into account are the impact of the increase in money wages on the aggregate price level (or on inflation) as emphasized in Chapter 3, and the reactions of the government to reduce inflation which may hurt labour. If firms are assumed to (at least partially) mark up costs, an increase in money wages will create inflationary pressures which in turn will to a greater or lesser extent negatively affect the real wage. On the other hand, unions might be aware that in certain circumstances, the acceleration of inflation brings about pressures to adopt deflationary policies – with undesired effects on employment. These two 'boomerang effects' may constrain the attitudes of the union.

[b] The union will certainly face opposition from the firm or group of firms with which it is negotiating. Firms have a basic joint objective: to increase as much as possible the profit per unit sold (profit margin) and the number of units it can sell. The product of the two determines the amount of sales proceeds and, given the costs of production, the level of profits. There is a clear trade-off between the two objectives mentioned, that is, the greater the profit margin, *ceteris paribus*, the smaller the size of the clientèle. Firms try to maximize profits (sale proceeds net of costs), and hence, given the market constraints, will obviously resist increases in wage costs. The goods market poses a constraint for the firm, and the more strict the constraint, the greater the willingness of the firm to resist wage increases, and to impose conflict costs on unions.

[c] Finally, the bargaining power of the union depends on the support it has from its members, or the degree of workers'

militancy as stressed in Chapter 4. Here it is important to differentiate between the union and the union members (workers), on the one hand, and between militancy and bargaining power on the other hand. The union negotiates in the name of the workers, and must therefore represent their interests. If it does not, it loses bargaining power for it lacks support for its actions. On the other hand, militancy and labour mobilization only enhance the unions' bargaining power if unions and workers have the same purposes and agree on the strategies. A Wildcat strike is a good example of a situation in which the level of militancy is very high, but the union has lost control over the workers (due to differences in either purposes or strategies), and also the right to speak in their names, in which case its bargaining power is obviously very small.

Constraints [a], [b], and [c] are affected by a number of structural, institutional and conjunctural factors to which we now turn. In terms of the first set of constraints (listed under [a]), the following factors seem to be of some relevance:

[a.1] The impact of wage negotiations on inflation obviously depends on the 'size' of the negotiating party or the degree of centralization of wage bargaining. The greater the degree of centralization of negotiations, and hence the relative size of the negotiating party and weight in the formation of the aggregate price level, the greater the inflationary effect of wage increases.

[a.2] The real wage of a certain group of workers depends as much on their money wage as on the money wages of other workers in the economy, for the greater the increase in money wages in other sectors, the greater will be the average price level, and the lower the real wage of the group under consideration. Hence the union must take into account (the expected) level of wages in other sectors when negotiating its own money wage.[5] The degree of *synchronization* in the formation of wages in the economy plays an important role in shaping the attitude of unions and workers for the greater the degree of dis-synchronization, the greater the uncertainty concerning the level of wages in other sectors. When uncertainty is large, and the risk of falling behind the average is thus large, workers try to protect the purchasing power of their future income by augmenting their demands for wage increases. When wages are set in synchronous fashion (which is usually the case when the degree of centralization is high), or a certain sector plays the role of a 'pattern setter', the level of uncertainty is reduced, and the incentive to take precautionary measures diminishes.

[a.3] No matter how centralized and synchronized negotiations actually are, and the effect on aggregate inflation of wage increases in a given sector actually is, the attitude of the union will only be influenced by this factor if it realizes or if it is *aware* of the consequences of the wage bargain. Of course, the greater the size of the union, the greater the likelihood that it will be aware and hence consider the macroeconomic effects of its activities. In particular, in countries in which negotiations take place at very high levels, union leaders are clearly aware of the aggregate impacts of wage negotiations. They tend, therefore, to internalize the costs of the externalities created by the negotiations. Small unions, on the other hand, usually are not aware of the macroeconomic impacts of their demands.

In terms of the second constraint [b], or the goods market constraint:

[b.1] It is reasonable to assume that the elasticity of demand of the negotiating firms falls as the level of centralization of negotiations increases at the industry level. Firms can enter into collusive action and clients have a smaller number of substitutes to choose from as the level of centralization increases.[6] This obviously implies that the market constraints become less stringent as the degree of centralization increases, and that firms' willingness to engage in conflict with workers falls thus reducing the costs of overindexation.

[b.2] If we look either at a particular industry or at a national economy, the size of the market constraint will depend on the level of protection from external competitors and the degree of trade dependence (that is, necessity to export). Protected and domestic-oriented industries face smaller market constraints than unprotected and export-oriented industries.

We finally turn to the third set of constraints [c] associated with the labour organization and incentives for workers' militancy:

[c.1] The degree of centralization of the labour movement may be an important factor in shaping unions' attitudes in wage bargaining. *Ceteris paribus*, small unions are weaker than large unions. Industry unions control the supply of labour to a set of firms and have more power than firm unions. The centralization of the union movement increases its bargaining power. This is not meant to deny the fact that certain small unions in decentralized systems may be very powerful. The argument is only that the bargaining power of a (legitimate) union tends to be greater the larger the number of its members. The existence of active central unions which support industry and local unions in their negotiations, and maintain ties with political parties, represents yet another important element in understanding the conditions of wage restraint.

[c.2] Policies which protect the workers' income from shocks or the conditions of the economy – or, in short, insulate the workers' income from market fluctuations – tend to reduce labour militancy. In advanced OECD economies, and in Western Europe in particular, the increase in social spending, or the increase in the 'social wage', can be seen as a response to labour militancy and the rise of the socialist parties and, as a consequence, an important factor in taming labour militancy. In the case of inflation-prone economies, wage laws have an important role protecting real wages against inflation. If the policy is effective in protecting wages, the incentives for mobilization during bargaining periods are reduced. As argued in Chapter 3, both the degree of indexation to past inflation and the length of the indexation period are important in determining the effectiveness of the wage policy. Low degrees of indexation and long indexation periods imply great vulnerability of wages to inflationary shocks, and thus create incentives for mobilization and conflict.

[c.3] Instability is also a factor to be considered. When recent history is marked by recurrent inflationary shocks, changes in policies and rules of the game, leading to erratic movements of the real wage, there is an incentive for workers to take preemptive actions during negotiations. Such actions aim to increase wages as an insurance against shocks at the cost of more mobilization.

[c.4] Finally, the conditions of the labour market as represented by the rate of unemployment affect negatively the level of militancy and the capacity of unions to mobilize workers, thus reducing their bargaining power.

Conditions for Wage Restraint

The discussion in the previous section provides a guide for the analysis of the factors accounting for wage restraint. National experiences are the outcome of a myriad of interrelated factors, but some of these factors are certainly more salient than others. Comparative analyses of national experiences in which outstanding factors are highlighted have proved to be instructive exercises. The analysis of the unions' aims and attitudes under different circumstances is used in what follows to sort out the alternative 'ideal cases' discussed in the literature on industrial relations and macroeconomic performance. The ideal cases can be seen as resulting from the combination of certain conditions associated with different sub-sets of constraints to the unions' actions. Table 5.1 summarizes these conditions.

A careful analysis of the table reveals a fundamental inconsistency between the conditions for wage restraint. There is a clear contradiction between the two first conditions, that is, [A.1+A.2+A.3] and [B.1+C.1]. The two sets of conditions are associated with two different industrial relations paradigms, namely, the societal corporatist and the pluralist paradigms, respectively. In what follows we address the theoretical and conceptual roots of these two paradigmatic cases. This discussion will serve as the basis for the introduction of two hybrid cases which in our view portray the institutional arrangements found in many market economies, and in the Brazilian economy in particular.

Table 5.1 Conditions for wage restraint

[A.1 + A.2 + A.3]	Negotiations at national or near-national level and/or synchronization in wage setting
[B.1 + C.1]	Small unions and decentralized/localized negotiations
[B.2 + C.4]	Trade dependency and (threat of) unemployment
[C.2 + C.3]	Insulation of workers' income from shocks and market fluctuations. Stable rules of the game and government/employers' credibility

Societal Corporatism

The notions of societal corporatism [Schmitter, 1971] and neo-corporatism [Crouch, 1985] are rather diffuse.[7] They involve different aspects of interest representation including the degrees of centralization of the union and employers' movements and of collective bargaining, relations between the labour movement and political parties, and participation of labour leaders in government. However, an outstanding underlying argument in favour of the cooperative behaviour of agents in corporatist systems is that the smaller the number of powerful players in the political market the greater the damages which individual groups can inflict on others, and therefore the greater the incentives for cooperation. The obstruction capacity of the groups, and the detrimental aggregate or social effects of each group's actions, are so huge that the benefits of cooperation increasingly dominate the costs of conflict. Not only that, but some would also argue that by exploring the gains of cooperation, agents could also transform a 'zero-sum game' into a 'positive-sum game' [Korpi and Shalev, 1979, p. 172].

95

In the industrial relations arena, in most of the countries which today constitute the representatives of the ideal corporatist case, the massive conflict (between workers and employers) that characterized centralized systems was replaced by cooperative actions aimed at long-term goals which are seen as beneficial to both groups. The centralization of the union movement, which in most European countries took place after the First World War, can be seen as an attempt by union leaders to expand their bargaining power in the political market.[8] The consequences of the political action of centralized workers' movements are appreciable: the participation of labour representatives in political parties and the government, and the adoption of normative interventions of the State in labour relations, such as the establishment of minimum wages, maximum working hours, unemployment benefits, and social security schemes, are the most prominent examples.

As a result of the participation of organized labour in the political market, and indeed in local and national governments, cooperative rather than conflictual relations between unions and employers have developed. To be sure, a major exchange between workers and employers has preceded the inauguration of the cooperative system – an exchange of workers' protection against market fluctuations for lower militancy. The attainment of long-term goals at the cost of short-term sacrifices is also seen as a consequence of the 'social-democratic pact'.

Centralized and synchronized wage bargaining is also seen as an important characteristic of corporatist systems, and indeed a major factor – together with the cooperative compromise – in explaining wage restraint. In this connection, the social bounds imposed on agents' attitudes by a particular institutional arrangement, namely, centralized bargaining, is very important. The combination of constraints A.1, A.2 and A.3 is central for the explanation of wage restraint in corporatist systems: because the bargaining parties have a 'socially relevant size' their attitudes have an immediate effect on aggregate variables.[9] Immediate or individual gains have to be weighted against the medium- and long-term and social losses. In the case of fully centralized and synchronized bargains, the intertemporal net gains become clearly perceived by the agents, who therefore act accordingly. Where negotiations are only centrally coordinated, or parallel but decentralized, bargains may give rise to wage drift, depending on the sizes of the second and third tiers negotiating parties, the net intertemporal effects might *not* be taken into account because agents may not be aware of the losses, or have difficulties in assessing them. Where negotiations are decentralized and/or scattered over time, and the negotiating parties are small, the level of awareness will tend to be small.[10]

Much ink has been used to provide empirical evidence that the corporatist system (crudely typified by centralized union organization *cum* centralized/synchronized wage bargaining) is conducive to wage restraint. To summarize the central arguments we consider the works of Crouch (1985) and Cameron (1985).[11] The common aspect of these analyses is an attempt to show that diversity in economic performance among advanced OECD economies after the mid-1970s is closely correlated to industrial relations institutions.

Crouch's central argument is that the relation between union density and inflationary pressures must be mediated by institutional variances; and that the record of corporatist countries with respect to the relation between unionization and inflation (and the Phillips curve trade-off) is superior to that of pluralist systems.[12] Crouch summarizes his findings with respect to wage restraint as follows:

> the extraordinary rise in inflation during the mid-1970s, as well as the difference among national rates of price acceleration, is better explained by industrial relations forces than just by prior inflation alone. This is compatible with the hypothesis that organized labour used its strength to secure short-term protection from the commodity price shocks, except to the extent that neo-corporatist structures led it to pursue strategies more compatible with longer-term price stability. ... Where there is social consensus (which might be secured by corporatist institutions) there will be relatively rapid adaptation of real wages to economic developments, and therefore less inflation. (pp. 124–5)

The work of Cameron (1985) attacks the dominant view according to which there exists a trade-off between inflation and unemployment. He uses a cross-country correlation analysis to show that, contrary to the conventional wisdom, among advanced industrial countries, those in which the acceleration of inflation was smaller were also the ones in which unemployment did not increase significantly after the oil shocks of 1974 and 1979. Also, he shows that money-wage inflation and real wage increases took place where the degree of workers' militancy (as measured by strike activity) was greater. The conclusion is that real wage restraint is positively associated with low levels of militancy, money wage and price inflation, and unemployment. Cameron further argues that corporatist institutions – for example, organizational unity of the labour movement and role ascribed to central union in wage bargaining – and dominance of leftist parties in the government are the common features of countries with the best macroeconomic record.

Pluralism

The pluralist ideal case is best portrayed by the 'competitive system' which plays a paradigmatic role in the neoclassical economics literature. Where agents are too small to affect the market, the forces of supply and demand at the industry level fix the money wage and price of output. In the idealized atomistic system, firms are small and take the price of the goods they produce as given. Faced with a given price, and with a money wage determined by supply and demand for labour at the industry level, the firm fixes the optimal levels of output and employment. The interaction between the actions of the individual agent and the market forces which ultimately determine prices is not spelled out in the competitive paradigm. Indeed, this is a widely recognized weakness of the model which relies on the figure of a ghost called the 'Walrasian auctioneer' to collect demands and supplies of millions of agents, to determine eventually, through a trial and error process, the competitive equilibrium prices.

In order to make sense from an empirical perspective, the competitive system has to be modified. In the economics jargon, a certain degree of 'imperfection' must be introduced. The demand curve faced by producers (an individual firm or a group of them producing similar goods) is not perfectly elastic and certain oligopolist factors such as fewness and product differentiation are taken into account. These modifications imply that a certain degree of discretion in the formation of prices is allowed for. In the labour market, labour segmentation due to differences in general abilities and specific skills as well as factors influencing the bargaining power of unions, lead to modifications in the outcome resulting from the forces of 'supply and demand' or the 'auction market.'[13] The determination of wages and prices will ultimately depend on the goods market constraints (or firms' degree of freedom to alter prices) and the bargaining power of the union and the firm(s).[14]

Where wage bargains take place at very decentralized levels, the power of confederations and federations is negligible, and direct negotiations between local unions and the firm are the ultimate determinants of wages. Under these circumstances, conditions B.1 and C.1 hold, and wage restraint results from the fact that competitive pressures put a cap on price and wage increases. In pluralist systems, therefore, the market imposes bounds on individual agents' actions.

Faced with an adverse shock, like the oil shocks of 1974 and 1979 or productivity slowdowns which tend to reduce the demand for labour, economies with pluralist institutions would respond with brisk real wage moderation. As a result, neither inflation nor the level of unemployment would suffer considerable increases. According to empirical analyses, conducted by Bruno and Sachs (1985) and Klau and Mittelstadt (1986), real wage flexibility in the case of the US, for example, resulted not only from the decentralized and dis-synchronized pattern of wage bargaining, but also from the fact that there is a low degree of unionization and a 'rapid inflow into the labour force of young persons and women prepared to accept employment at low wages' (Klau and Mittelstadt, p. 25). The low degree of wage indexation to inflation and the presence of multi-year contracts are repeatedly mentioned as important factors as well.

Flexible wage differentials also account for rapid adjustment to shocks which hit different sectors with different strength. Again, in empirical studies it has been found that the degree of relative wage flexibility is greater in the US than in European countries, and it has been argued that this could explain the greater degree of real wage flexibility (see Klau and Mittelstadt). Bell and Freeman (1987) have noted, however, that although it is true that the US is unique in this respect – indeed, it is the only OECD advanced economy in which sectoral wage dispersion has increased – relative wage flexibility has not really worked to generate more employment. The increase in wage dispersion is associated with industry-specific conditions and not with changes in the sectoral patterns of demand and supply for labour. Quite the contrary from expected, wages have been growing in sectors in which productivity has gone up, and falling (though not as much) where productivity has been falling. As a result, the net effect of the increase in wage dispersion cannot be seen as a positive factor in increasing the level of employment.

Intermediate and Hybrid Systems

The corporatist and pluralist systems discussed are really limit-cases, and can be seen as two poles of a spectrum on which other relevant systems exist. The 'hybrid cases' preserve some of the characteristics of the pure cases, but at the same time present certain distortions. In what follows we address three sources of modifications to the pure cases, and then build a taxonomy of systems based on two attributes: the level of centralization of collective bargains and the degree of synchronization of wage negotiations.

The three modifications to the pure cases are the following:

[i] The typical level of negotiation may be intermediary between the firm and the economy as a whole. When bargains take place at high levels of aggregation at the industry level, or at the industry level itself, some special features arise. As the size of the negotiating party increases the elasticity of demand falls because the 'good' now comprises a wider range of substitutes (see Calmfors and Driffill, 1988). Not only that but the possibility of collusion increases the firms' market power. On the other hand, the bargaining power of the union(s) tends to increase in direct relation to the size of the labour supply which it controls.[15] The slackening of the market constraint, and resulting increase in the market power of firms, and the increase in the bargaining power of unions, tend to reduce the bounds of wage (and price) increases.[16] From the point of view of the pluralist paradigm, the increase in the level of aggregation of negotiations at the industry level introduces an injurious 'imperfection' in the system.

In terms of the corporatist system, the reduction in the level of bargaining (in relation to the centralized system) is also damaging for it reduces the level of awareness of the agents concerning the aggregate consequences of their actions. From a comparative perspective, therefore, the intermediate case is inferior in relation to both the pluralist case and the corporatist case. Industry level negotiations are seen as conducive to wage inflation and price inflation.

[ii] Decentralized negotiations do not necessarily imply dis-synchronization for bargains may occur simultaneously. On the other hand, where centralized bargaining exists, there is space for the effects of assynchronity as second- and third-layer negotiations usually coexist with economy-wide bargains. In sum, conditions A.1 and A.2 do not mutually imply each other, and hence another source of variation with respect to the two pure cases is the possibility of 'centralized but assynchronic' and 'decentralized but synchronic' negotiations. The former is in fact implicit where corporatist institutions predominate.

Both centralization and synchronization are seen as important coordinating instruments and factors accounting for wage restraint. The gains stemming from centralization have already been discussed. Synchronization in turn mitigates the level of uncertainty concerning the future path of wages in different sectors of the economy, and hence reduces the incentives for unions to take preemptive actions against possible reductions in real wages. It is important to note that neither centralization nor synchronization are sufficient conditions to prevent nominal wage increases. Wage drift can occur in both cases when the patterns set by the nation-wide bargain or a pattern setter, respectively, are not respected in local negotiations.

[iii] The role of central unions or confederations in collective bargaining also affects the system of industrial relations. Two aspects seem important in this connection. The first is the extent to which confederations participate in bargains. In some countries the participation is negligible if it exists at all; in others they play the role of a consulting agent in providing the negotiating unions with advice and expertise; in others they negotiate in the name of the unions. In the first and second cases the power of the central unions is limited but in the third case unions may not have the right to renegotiate at the local or plant level issues negotiated at higher levels.

Another important aspect refers to the degree of centralization of the union movement and the bargaining process. Where a single confederation exists the prospects of concerted policies, and hence macroeconomic coordination, are greater. Where more than one confederation exists, and the cleavages are political, the actions of central unions may be rather disrupting not only because of differences in strategies, but also because they make tripartite accords much more difficult. Where the confederations are weak and insignificant, their overall role in collective bargaining is negligible, and the prospects of concerted policies are non-existent.

Table 5.2 is an attempt to take stock of the previous discussion. It considers two attributes of wage setting-negotiations, namely, the degree of centralization (high, intermediate and low) and the degree of synchronization (high and low). High degrees of centralization and synchronization characterize the corporatist system whereas the symmetric case characterizes the pluralist system. High and negligible degrees of unification of the union movement, respectively, are implicit in the two limit cases.

There are two hybrid cases of some interest. In the Hybrid I case, the degree of centralization of negotiations is intermediate (or low) but the degree of synchronization is high – thus providing a significant coordinating element to the system. The role of pattern setters is important in this system. In Hybrid II, the predominant level of negotiation is intermediary and the degree of synchronization is low. This is a system with very problematic features because all the coordinating mechanisms are absent.

Table 5.2 Patterns of wage bargains

		Level of centralization		
		High	Intermediate	Low
Level of synchronization	High	Corporatist	Hybrid	***
	Low	***	Hybrid	Pluralist

During the 1980s a general trend towards decentralization of negotiations has been noted in all advanced industrialized countries.

The requirements of greater flexibility of wages and labour processes in the face of new developments in technologies and of the economic crisis have led employers to push for decentralized bargains. The tendency is much clearer in the US and UK than in other countries.[17] Where a tradition of relatively centralized negotiations (either at the industry level or at the national level) exists, the change has been much slower. In fact, industrial relations institutions have shown an impressive degree of inertia even in the face of employers' and some governments' attempts to change them (see Treu, 1987).

The slots in which Sweden, Austria, Finland, Denmark and Norway, on the one hand, and the US and Canada, on the other, fit in Table 5.2 is incontrovertible. The first group forms the core of the corporatist system, whereas the second is distinctively pluralist. More difficult to classify are the cases of the Netherlands, Belgium, West Germany, Italy, France, the UK and Japan. In order to illustrate the hybrid cases we shall direct our attention to the cases of Belgium, France and Japan.

Japan is usually seen as a typical pluralist case. Calmfors and Driffill (1988, p. 16) for example contend that 'as to Japan, there are several national confederations of labour but their coordinating roles are minor, and the actual negotiations take place exclusively at the enterprise level.' It is quite true that the confederations play a minor role and that, ultimately, negotiations take place at the firm level, but there are two characteristics of the Japanese system which differentiate it quite dramatically from the American and Canadian systems.

On the one hand, the role of pattern setting is very important in establishing the guidelines for negotiations. On the other, there is a preparation involving major industry-level federations for what is called the spring wage offensive (*Shunto*) in which macroeconomic issues and other national themes are taken into account. More important, however, is the fact that all negotiations take place around a certain period, that is, the degree of synchronization is extremely high.

The decentralized nature of collective bargaining in Japan has been over-emphasized in the literature. Again, although it is true that formal negotiations take place at the enterprise level, intense informal negotiations at higher levels seem to play a decisive role in shaping local agreements. Employers and union confederation leaders meet frequently with government officials to exchange views on major national issues.

Table 5.3 Hybrid cases

	Belgium	France	Japan
Unemployment[a]	11.0	7.2	2.2
Inflation[b]	7.6	12.9	5.2
Okun Index[c]	17.0	16.9	9.1
Strike activity	156.0	278.0	71.0
Scope of wage bargaining	Interm.	Interm.	Interm.
Synchronization of wage bargaining	Low	Low	High

[a] Percentage of labour force, average 1980–82. *Source*: Cameron (1985).
[b] Annual, 1980–82. *Source*: Cameron (1985).
[c] Okun misery index is the sum of the rates of unemployment and inflation, in this case the average levels between 1974 and 1985. *Source*: Calmfors and Driffill (1988).

Industry-wide federations of enterprise unions not only establish the guidelines for local negotiations, but indeed, as noted by Shirai (in Windmuller et al., 1987, p. 243),

> in *de facto* negotiations the representatives of industrial federations of unions do not act as bargaining agents for the affiliated enterprise unions, but negotiate annual wage increases informally and directly with the top management of leading corporations. ... The most typical case is that of the centralized bargaining practiced since 1959 in the steel industry between the leaders of the Japanese Federation of Iron and Steel Workers' Unions (*Tekkororen*) and the management

of the five major steel corporations. ... This has become the normal method of
wage fixing in the iron and steel industry and has set the pattern for the wage
settlement procedure followed in some other major industries.

Shirai also notes that the leadership of the *Shunto* offensive is
dominated by the federations of the iron and steel, shipbuilding,
automobile and electrical appliances industries, and that although
the role of the National Joint Committee for the Spring Offensive
is informal, the bargaining with employers' representatives

has practically the same effect as more systematic procedures of industry-wide or
multi-industry negotiations since the industries concerned are closely related and
exert a decisive influence on wage settlements in other branches such as
chemicals, metal engineering, private and national railways, telecommunications,
and postal services, and national and local civil services. (p. 244)

The guidelines are usually followed at the enterprise level. At
the industry level, in general the leading firm sets its wage, and the
others tend to follow the leader because this at the same time saves
bargaining costs and is in accordance with the principle of 'wage
justice' (see Takanashi et al., 1989, p. 15).

It seems that to place Japan among the pluralist countries is
very misleading. Indeed, in doing so the important coordinating
elements of the Japanese system, namely, pattern setting and
synchronization, are relegated to a secondary status, and the
compliance of local negotiations with the guidelines established at
higher levels comes to be seen inaccurately as a consequence of
'smallness' and market forces.

In France, the level of synchronization of wage bargains is very
low, which implies that the conditions for coordination in this
respect are non-existent. As for the level of wage bargaining, it
usually takes place at the industry level for the fixation of
guidelines – which becomes the minimum level – and then
renegotiations at the enterprise level determine the actual wage.[18]
Another aspect of the French case which deserves attention is the
role of central unions, split into political lines, which tend to act
independently from each other and from the government, thus
reducing the level of standardization and coordination of the
system. This is the typical case in which a few powerful agents
without much commitment with the aggregate consequences of their
acts can create significant economic and even social disarray. In

such cases, neither coordination through concertation nor the discipline imposed by the impetus of the market seem to impose wage restraint.

In Belgium, negotiations take place at different levels depending on the industry: at the national inter-industry level (until 1975), at the national industry level, and at the regional and enterprise levels. High-level negotiations usually set minimum standards which can be renegotiated at lower levels. However, after the mid-1970s, as a result of the economic crisis which hit the Belgian economy very strongly, inter-industry negotiations have not been concluded. Blanpain (in Windmuller et al., 1987) points out that 'as a consequence of the crisis, the difference between the stronger and the weaker sectors of the economy has become more pronounced, so that an overall agreement under which the trade unionists in the stronger sectors risk losing their comparative advantages has become a less realistic proposition' (p. 183). In some industries (such as textiles, insurance and retailing) national agreements are still the rule, but in others (metalworking) local agreements have prevailed.

Much as in the French case, in Belgium there are different levels of bargaining depending on the industry, and negotiations have obviously not been synchronized. As a response to the lack of negotiations at the inter-industry national level, and increasing reduction in the degree of coordination, since 1981 the government and the parliament have imposed mandatory restrictions on wage increases, which have led to a certain degree of real wage moderation, indeed real wage reductions in some years. Since then, collective bargains have been restricted to other issues among which the reduction in work time and job security are prominent.

The cases of Japan, Belgium and France are illustrative of the fact that differences in the levels of negotiation and synchronization of wage setting give rise to interesting hybrid cases. In Japan, negotiations formally take place at the enterprise level but informal negotiations at higher levels, pattern setting and synchronization play an important part in the determination of the actual level of wages. In France and Belgium, negotiations take place at different levels but the role of inter-industry negotiations has been eroded by the crisis in the last ten to fifteen years and the degree of synchronization and pattern setting is very low. These differences tend to imply that the potential for wage restraint in Japan is considerably greater than in the two European countries, and the facts confirm this hypothesis.

Both Calmfors and Driffill (1988) and Freeman (1989) argue that there exists a hump-shaped relation between the degree of centralization of negotiations and wage restraint. The conditions for wage restraint hold either when negotiations take place at a very high level or a very low level. Intermediate systems are bound to excessive wage increase and, hence, a severe trade-off between inflation and unemployment.[19] The hump-shaped pattern results from a lack of coordinating mechanisms at intermediate levels of bargaining.

We would argue that there are other factors accounting for the degree of coordination and wage restraint. As noted above, the degree of synchronization of negotiations or the existence of pattern setters affect the level of coordination. If negotiations take place at the industry level (such as we would argue is the case in Japan) but the degree of synchronization is high, the level of coordination will be greater than in cases in which wage bargains are scattered over time and pattern-setting industries do not exist (as in France and Belgium). A greater degree of synchronization is thus likely to shift the real wage curve downwards as shown in Figure 5.1.

Workers' Militancy

For the workers, militancy is a (costly) response to their discontent. Under normal circumstances, a reduction in the level of dissatisfaction will lead to a reduction in the level of activism. Militancy can be dampened by repression or by the imposition of economic costs such as the threat of unemployment. However, the use of political or economic costs as weapons to reduce labour militancy have long been (partially) replaced in industrialized countries by the introduction of social benefits which protect workers against market fluctuations. As the risk or costs to the worker of being unemployed are reduced, the incentives to mobilize and the levels of industrial conflicts tend to fall. As noted by Esping-Andersen and Korpi (1985), social policies were introduced in European countries in two steps. First as an attempt by the ruling classes to preserve social stability (social reforms imposed 'from above'), and then through the actions of unions and social democratic parties.[20]

Therborn (1986), in the same vein, argues that in some industrialized countries an institutionalized commitment to full employment developed either as a result of 'the concern of certain bourgeoisies with social stability', or as a result of 'the wish of strong labour movements for full employment' (p. 111). Quite clearly, the propositions put forward by these authors imply that social reforms and the commitment to full employment were the outcome of a process of political struggle in which workers' militancy and organization played an important part. To the workers, unemployment benefits and the government's commitment to full employment programmes are two major shields against market fluctuations. To the ruling classes, they imply a redistribution of income in favour of workers in exchange for social order.

However misleading cross-country comparisons may be, it seems that a negative correlation can be identified between unemployment compensation and (commitment to full) employment,[21] on the one hand, and labour militancy (as measured by strike activity), on the other hand. In Table 5.4, those countries where the rate of unemployment was relatively low in the early 1980s and unemployment benefits are higher are precisely those where the level of strike activity was lowest, namely, Austria, Japan, Norway, Sweden and Switzerland. Canada, Australia, France, Italy, the UK and the US are on the opposite pole of the spectrum.

In inflation-prone economies, wage policies are an important source of protection to workers' income. As shown in Chapter 2, if wages are adjusted to inflation and the adjustment period is not too long, major wage reductions can be avoided. The protection of real wages against the acceleration of inflation and unemployment benefits plays a very similar role: they both insulate the income of workers from two variables (the price level and the rate of unemployment) which are out of their control. In this sense, wage policies designed to protect wages against inflation also tend to reduce the level of workers' militancy. The inverse is also true, that is, when wage controls aim at the reduction of inflation through forced wage restraint (reductions in real wages) they tend to increase militancy and conflict. That is why in many recent stabilization attempts in Latin America, when the government tries to reduce inflation by de-indexing wages or increasing the length

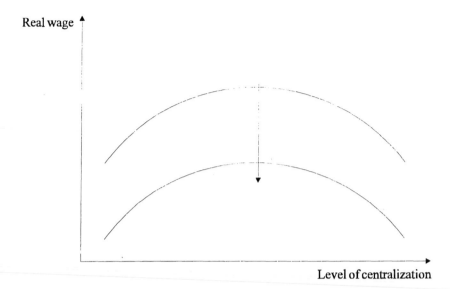

Figure 5.1 Centralization and synchronization of bargains

of the indexation period the level of conflict immediately increases.

Trade Dependency and Policy Accommodation

Given the institutional setting in which wages are determined, there are other subsidiary factors usually seen as relevant in explaining wage restraint. One is the degree of trade dependency (B.2 in Table 5.1) and the other is the degree of policy accommodation of inflationary pressures which partly determines the actual levels of inflation and unemployment (given the 'position' of the Phillips curve) and indeed influences the trade-off itself between the two variables.

Trade dependency – or the extent to which an economy depends on foreign trade – is both a matter of structural (given) constraint and (choice of) development strategy. In connection with the theme of wage determination, economic openness is important for it sets external limits to increases in prices, and thus affects the behaviour of employers in wage bargains. A firm which exports 100% of its output is bound to set its price equal to the international level, and therefore is willing to restrict wage increases more than other firms which only sell in the domestic market and have their market shares protected against foreign competition. The former is the case of a significant proportion of the firms in small open economies such as the Scandinavian countries, Austria, the Netherlands and Belgium. In comparing these economies with the large industrialized economies, Katzenstein (1983) notes that they:

> are unusually open to and dependent on a global economy which is beyond their control. The economic structure of the small European states is less diversified than that of the large states. Furthermore the small European states depend heavily on the import of investment goods and other products for which their small domestic markets simply do not offer large economies of scale. Instead they seek these economies of scale through a specialization in their exports. (p. 101)

Katzenstein and others (Lange, 1981 and Lloyd and Flanagan, 1971, for example) have argued that there is an important relation stemming from trade dependency to corporatist structures and wage restraint. Since wage and price restraint are imperative in open economies, the incentives for cooperation between labour and capital (in some cases under the leadership of the government) are very large.[22]

To a certain extent, openness is also a question of choice. Indeed, the degree of trade liberalization is a strategic issue being debated in many countries today. Large economies can seek an autonomous route (as Brazil and India have done) but the advantages of such an option have been scrutinized in recent years under the argument that the lack of competition discourages the incentives for innovations and the search for productivity gains. It also has the perverse effect of reducing the limits on wage and price increases. Policy accommodation is also an important factor in explaining the position of the curve depicted in Figure 5.1. As in the case of trade dependency, it is a question of choice but it has strong structural roots. In principle, the government can inhibit inflationary pressures by adopting a tight monetary and fiscal policy thus increasing the tension of the goods and labour markets constraints. However, the extent to which this is actually a choice is not very clear.

Governments are in principle autonomous and may have an idea of the relation between policy instruments and their outcomes. But in many circumstances, in the face of certain compromises (most prominently when some kind of concertation is in place), or as a result of limits imposed by side effects of non-accommodative policies, the government is incapable of applying the brakes. Situations of political stalemate, in which the government does not have the required support of major social agents to impose restrictive monetary policies, abound in history.[23]

Stabilization Policies

In this section we discuss the prospects of three broadly defined varieties of stabilization policies in the face of three different 'social systems' where the latter are predominantly characterized by their industrial relations structures. The reduction of inflation is assumed to be the primary goal of the policies. We look at three systems – Corporatist/Hybrid I, Pluralist and Hybrid II – and three stylized policies or 'solutions' – market policies, concerted incomes policies and non-negotiated incomes policies. We ask to what extent each of these policies is (ir)relevant, (in)feasible and (un)effective, and what is the level of costs (as measured by increases in unemployment, poverty and inequality) associated with each of them, in each of the three social scenarios. Table 5.5 summarizes the suggested outcomes. Governments use restrictive monetary and fiscal policies to reduce the market power of economic agents, and thus curb the creation of inflationary pressures. In order to successfully implement this kind of policy the government must be prepared to face the (political and electoral) losses stemming from the dis-satisfaction of the losers – and there are many in the short run though not necessarily so many in the long run. The existence of safety nets (for example, unemployment benefits) mitigates the costs associated with the policy. Depending on the extent to which agents' market powers depend on the conditions of the economy – a condition which ultimately hinges on structural and institutional factors – the required costs to segments of the society may be large or small. In pluralist systems this type of policy is usually feasible and efficacious, and the social costs relatively small. The prospects of market solutions are thinner in situations in which there is a large number of powerful agents, such

Table 5.4 Commitment to full employment, unemployment and benefits and workers' militancy

	Rate of unemployment[a]	Unemployment benefits[b]	Strike activity[c]
Belgium	13.9	–	156
Canada	11.8	42.9	707
Denmark	10.6	86.0	148
Netherlands	13.7	–	22
UK	13.0	32.0	375
Average	10.0	53.6	283
Australia	9.9	–	427
Finland	6.1	42.0	258
France	8.4	42.9	278
Germany	8.0	67.4	28
Italy	9.8	17.4	849
USA	9.5	36.3	411
Average	11.5	41.2	391
Austria	4.1	–	10
Japan	2.6	68.9	71
Norway	3.3	59.0	28
Sweden	3.5	93.0	95
Switzerland	0.9	–	1
Average	8.1	76.6	41

[a] Percentage of labour force in 1983. *Source*: Therborn (1986).
[b] Percentage of average wage. *Source*: Therborn (1986).
[c] Working days lost in industrial disputes per 1000 in total labour force. *Source*: ILO as reported by Cameron (1985)

*Table 5.5 Varieties of stabilization approaches in
    alternative social scenarios*

	Corporatism or Hybrid I	Pluralism	Hybrid II
Market solution	Relatively unimportant	Effective	Very costly
Concerted incomes policy	Effective	Infeasible	Infeasible
Non-negotiated incomes policy	Unrealistic	Ineffective	Ineffective

as in the case of Hybrid II systems.[24] In these cases, agents are able
to resist reductions in their standard of living, thus requiring a
greater injection of market repression to respond to the policy.
Hence the trade-off between inflation and unemployment tends to
be greater.[25] The conditions for concerted incomes policies can be
seen in terms of three headings: institutional, political and economic
conditions. Institutionally, it has become quite accepted that
centralized union and employers' structures and centralized
bargaining are very important. Tarantelli (1983, 1986, 1987) has
argued quite convincingly that not only is the centralization of
negotiations an important condition, but also the level of
synchronization of negotiations. As noted above, these two
conditions do not mutually imply each other. In the case of the
Nordic European counties and Austria both centralization and
synchronization are present. But in the case of Japan, for example,
the degree of centralization is not that high, but wages are
determined almost simultaneously and pattern setters play an
important role.[26]

From the political point of view, the extent to which labour is
represented, and the degree of inclusion of labour in the state (both
through political parties and the administration itself) are usually
seen as important factors accounting for the feasibility and efficacy

113

of negotiated incomes policy. Cameron (1985) notes that the presence of labour and social democratic parties in governments is an important element in explaining the relative success of some countries in dealing with the crisis. Regini (1985, p. 128) argues that militancy moderation is usually exchanged for unions' participation in policy-making:

> The state devolves portions of its decision-making authority to trade unions, by allowing them to play a part in policy formation and implementation and, thus, to gain advantage from the material and symbolic resources which the state can distribute. In return for this, trade unions deliver their indirect political power to the state by guaranteeing consensus and by drawing on their own resources to ensure the legitimacy, effectiveness and efficiency of state action.

Where unions do not participate in the political market, and hence are not involved in political exchange, the best strategy is to explore to the limit their bargaining power in the economic arena. The result, depending again on structural and institutional factors, may be lack of wage moderation, on the one hand, and the infeasibility of concerted incomes policy, on the other.

Mutual credibility between the actors and legitimacy of the leadership (which imply compliance of the rank and file with the agreed policy) are yet other important factors accounting for the possibility and potential efficacy of concerted incomes policies. When the recent history is one in which one of the negotiating parties has not complied with the agreed terms of the policy (either for lack of legitimacy or other reasons), the other parties will be less inclined to participate in cooperative actions.

Finally, there are economic conditions. Here the important theme is the degree to which participating agents agree on certain goals, and the related distribution of costs. A central area around which a certain degree of consensus is critical is the distribution of income seen not only in respect to the conflict between wages and profits, but also in reference to relative key prices and wages. Agents must agree on the distributive effects of the policy, and therefore the 'degree of acceptability' of the agents attached to different distributive outcomes must be roughly consistent. Let us take the real wage as a representative distributive variable. In Figure 5.2, the panel on the left depicts the degree of acceptability of employers associated with different levels of the real wage. *Ceteris paribus*, employers may be prepared to accept increases in the real wage, but the degree of acceptability falls as the real wage increases. On the right-hand panel, the workers' degree of acceptability is depicted. We have two cases to consider. If, for example, positive levels of acceptability of both employers and workers do not coincide (as in the case of curve A), the prospects of successful cooperation are nile. If, on the other hand, there is a range of wages to which positive degrees of acceptability of both employers and workers exist, the prospects become greater. Indeed, if a high degree of acceptability of both parties is associated with a certain level of the real wage, then an accord becomes possible.

In economies with high and accelerating inflation, it becomes very difficult to find a set of ranges of distributive variables to which reasonably high degrees of acceptability can be attached. Periods of inflationary surges are accompanied by large distributive fluctuations which in turn lead to episodes of distributive conflict. An attempt to establish a solution under such circumstances will find 'winners' trying to preserve their current positions, and 'losers' demanding significant changes in their positions. Hence the prospects of cooperation become very small.

Some special circumstances may create conditions for concertation. One is the existence of an external factor, such as foreign competition, which poses significant limits to the well-being of all agents . If recognized as a major element negatively affecting a majority of the agents, external threats can mitigate the force of conflicting interests, and favour cooperation. A situation of progressing crisis, which as a result of perverse negative feedback effects, ultimately hurts the interests of all groups, can also engender cooperation. However, as in the case of the external threat, the incentives to cooperate will only materialize if the agents become conscious of their inability to cope with the crisis in isolation, or more to the point, become conscious that the pay-off associated with the cooperative solution is greater than the pay-off associated with the exploration of individual market forces. A prisoner's dilemma situation is likely to prevent cooperation. This is true especially in cases in which the number of players is large enough to inhibit negotiations, and their market power is sufficiently large to create the illusion that free-riding is preferred to the cooperative outcome.

Given these conditions, it seems obvious that concertation is inconceivable in pluralist systems and hopeless in Hybrid II systems.

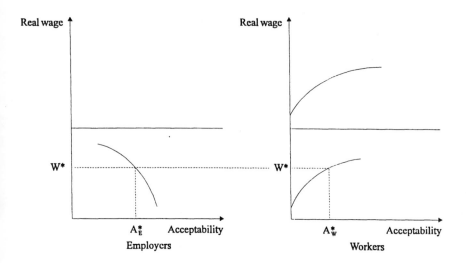

Figure 5.2 Distributive conflict

In circumstances in which there is sufficient centralization of interests representation, but the political or economic conditions do not apply, concertation is also very difficult.

A last policy approach to stabilization is the adoption of a non-negotiated incomes policy which usually takes the form of wage and price controls. That is, an attempt by the government to determine the 'desired' levels of prices and wages, and thus distribution and relative prices. All the problems faced by concerted incomes policy plus some others are present here. To be successful, this approach requires that the government has either coercive or persuasive instruments to force or convince the agents to comply with the guidelines. Authoritarian regimes have the coercive powers. Legitimate and popular governments have some persuasive appeal. But the incentives to free ride are always present and will tend to have undesirable consequences in the case where agents are relatively strong. Democratic governments can always use market instruments to force the agents to comply with the controls. But the bottom line is that the degree of difficulty becomes greater as we move from the pluralist to the Hybrid II system.

We conclude by noting that there are policies which are more or less appropriate depending on the extent to which the economy is closer to the pluralist or corporatist pole. Some policy approaches are simply infeasible under certain circumstances; others are feasible but vary in the degree of efficacy and costs attached to them depending on the circumstances. Finally, it is worth noting that in Hybrid II systems, market solutions are very costly, concerted policies are impossible, and non-negotiated incomes policies tend to have a low degree of efficacy. As a corollary we are led to conclude that if institutional designs are seen as a matter of social choice, intermediate cases should be avoided.

Concluding Notes

Economists and policy makers like to think that in the face of certain problems (inflation or unemployment, for example), there exists a universally valid and correct set of policy prescriptions which, if appropriately implemented, would resolve the maladies of the economy. Indeed, many of the diagnoses and prescriptions offered by international agencies such as the IMF and the World Bank are in this vein. The government is somehow seen as omnipotent and able to choose the right policies, and if it does not pursue them, it is argued that some kind of perversion (corruption being a good example here) exists in the system. More sophisticated analysis of the Latin American cases attribute the causes of the mismanagement of the economy to 'populism' – defined as the incapacity of the government to restrict its activities to its means, and therefore accommodating inconsistent demands.

In fact, it is not true that there exists a universal set of policies to cure macroeconomic diseases. Different policies are more or less appropriate according to historical and institutional given and conjunctural circumstances. Moreover, in face of certain constraints, some (or most or all) policies may prove to be undesirable, infeasible, or even worse, ineffective. In another paper, co-authored with Tariq Banuri (Amadeo and Banuri, 1991), we argued that

contrary to what is suggested by economists' monistic vision ... governments are neither all-powerful nor completely powerless in most areas of social activity. First, polities as well as governments are characterized by differentiation and tension, rather than by monolithicity of structure and function. In order to understand the functioning and consequences of social decision-making, it is important to replace monistic perspectives with more pluralistic views ... and to see policy-making as the constrained decisions of one among many actors operating in a situation of conflict and tension, rather than autonomous actions of an independent and omnipotent actor. (p. 3)

The case of populism, seen by some economists as a cultural aberration characteristic of Latin American social structures, can be seen as a response of weak governments in the face of conflicting interests of private actors. The weakness of the government really implies that it would be difficult, if not impossible, to preserve some kind of political support without creating inconsistent forces at the macroeconomic level. In such cases, in the place of adopting policies which would create the conditions for the achievement of certain goals under the restriction of some long-term constraints, the government maximizes its short-term political support at the cost of ultimately creating significant macroeconomic imbalances.

The case of exchange rate devaluations is paradigmatic in this respect. In face the of balance of payment imbalances in the early 1980s many governments in Latin America promoted 'maxi-devaluations' of the national currencies in order to induce changes in relative prices in favour of tradable sectors. Where actors (both firms and workers) in the non-tradable sectors were able to resist the loss in their real incomes, the policy led to the acceleration of inflation, ultimately defeating the primary objective of the policy. In many cases, in order to coordinate the aimed change in distribution, the government had to create deflationary pressures. In most cases, as in the case of Brazil, some degree of real devaluation of the currency was attained at the cost of greater unemployment and higher rates of inflation.

The arguments presented so far should not be interpreted as a nihilist manifesto. Certain sets of policies are more appropriate than others given the circumstances, and some may be quite successful. This is true in the case of many economies over considerable periods of time – the cases of the Nordic countries, West Germany and Japan in the last three or four decades are quite obvious in this respect. However, the successful stories must be seen in terms of the underlying circumstances in which the policies were implemented.

Notes

1. See Lipietz et al., 1990 for an analysis of the end of the post-war golden age.
2. See Rowthorn and Glyn (1990) for a detailed analysis of the differences in national experiences.
3. This is the view expressed, for example, by Bruno and Sachs (1985) in their influential book on the causes of stagnation in OECD economies.
4. See Bruno and Sachs (1985) and Blanchard and Summers (1986) for examples of economic analyses emphasizing institutional aspects of the labour market and capital–labour relations.
5. The notion that relative wages are the real concern of unions was first put forward by Keynes in his *General Theory*. There he argued that 'the struggle about money-wages primarily affects the *distribution* of the aggregate real wage between different labour-groups, and not its average amount per unit of employment, which depends ... on a different set of forces. The effect of combination on the part of a group of workers is to protect their *relative* real wage' (1936, p. 14).
6. This argument has been put forward by Calmfors and Driffill (1988) in their analysis of the role of the centralization of wage bargains on wage restraint.
7. For a critique of the notion of corporatism and its association with macroeconomic performance, see Therborn (1986).
8. Pizzorno (1978, p. 286) notes that 'on the side of unions, the creation of central bodies (federation, confederation, national council, Bund, etc) may be considered an elementary indicator of the emergence of a situation which implies exchange between political actors.'
9. The argument is put forward by Crouch (1985a) as follows:

   Social interests that are organized on a small, localized scale receive in full any distortions they produce in market processes but bear only a minute proportion of the general cost. ... The position of an organized interest at a national or near-national level will be completely different, as it will experience directly the negative effects of its disruptions – it can therefore be expected to take these effects into account. (p. 107)

10. However, as we shall note in the next section, other bounds to the agents' behaviour may apply.
11. In the economics literature, Bruno and Sachs (1985) come to conclusions which in essence are very similar to the ones of Crouch and Cameron.
12. Austria, Denmark, Finland, Netherlands, Norway, Sweden, Switzerland and West Germany.
13. These modifications do not alter the essence of the pluralist paradigm which is that small negotiating agents have small market power.
14. There are other characteristics of the pluralist system which deserve special attention. One is that because agents are small they do not care about the (small) aggregate effects of their actions. The other characteristic does not really stem from the ideal case itself but it is observable in countries in which other pluralist features exist, and that is the low level of politicization of the agents. Not only the links between the unions and federations are weak, but the ties between the union movement and parties are also very thin. Crouch describes as follows the pluralist ideal system:

    [atomized] actors do not take action with regard to any perception of a general interest; the market impersonally imposes on them conformity with a general interest. Further, as economic actors they are confined to acting within the sphere of economic relations, producing and exchanging goods and services in order to realize a goal of

119

profit maximization. They have no concern for general political questions, and no sense of group or common interest. (Crouch, 1985a, p. 108)

15. The change in the elasticity of demand as negotiations become more centralized is spelled out in detail by Calmfors and Driffill (1988, p. 33):

> As unions get larger, they acquire greater market power. In an individual firm, workers have little market power. Indeed, any isolated increase in the nominal wage results in a large employment fall, since the firm is unable to raise its output price unless all firms within the industry do so. But, if the union were to control labour supply to all firms in the industry, its market power would grow. Indeed, each firm within the industry has the same incentive to raise its output price which, therefore, rises in the whole industry. Substitution now occurs only in relation to firms outside the industry, and no firm faces a fall in demand relative to other firms in the same industry.

16. Crouch provides an interesting view of the relation between the market power of firms and the limits of wage increases:

> It is within oligopolies and in the public sector that unionization in most countries is strongest; and in these sectors unions are able to bid up wages, not entirely independently of the overall level of unemployment but with considerably less dependence than in a perfectly competitive system. Within the oligopolies, unions have thus been able to preempt for labor at least some of the fruits of market power produced by the concentration of industry, leading either to profit squeeze or, as prices finally rise, inflation. (Crouch, 1985a, p. 107)

17. The role of employers in reducing unions' membership and replacing collective bargaining by individual agreements is particularly prominent in the US.

18. Caire (in Windmuller et al., 1987) notes that as for the negotiation of wages, 'collective bargaining ... is conducted at the industry level, the general practice being to negotiate only minima which enterprises, by unilateral decision, may exceed' (p. 201). However, there are variations according to the sector:

> At the level of industry-wide negotiations, ... complete disorder reigns. Some industries negotiate at the national level (chemicals and textiles, for example) but others prefer the local level and rule out any national agreements (e.g. metalworking). Sometimes (as in the construction industry) the national agreement explicitly relegates some matters – including wages – to supplementary local agreements. At other times, wage scales are determined at the national level with perhaps some local codicils being added later. (p. 200)

19. In the face of the recent trend towards decentralization, the following argument put forward by Calmfors and Driffill (1988, p. 47) calls for some degree of prudence: 'The main point remains that what one should not do is to go only part of the way to a somewhat more decentralized system with, say, industry-level bargaining. In economies with wage setting at this level one should not resist tendencies to enterprise bargaining in order to preserve some coordination.'

20. Esping-Andersen and Korpi (1985, pp. 180–81):

> With only a few exceptions, the welfare states of Western nations developed up to 1945 as a result of social policy imposed 'from above', where the working class was the *object* of the concerns and worries of the traditional ruling elites. As a result of improved capabilities for collective action during the first post-war decades manifested, for example, in significantly higher levels of unionization and leftist voting, the representatives of the working class increased their influence in legislatures and governments. This improved power position then enabled social democratic parties to become ... the *subjects* of welfare state development.

21. Therborn (1986) argues that the only countries where the level of unemployment was kept low in the late 1970s and early 1980s were those in which a commitment to full employment existed: Austria, Japan, Sweden, Norway and Switzerland.

22. Referring to the small European economies, Katzestein (1983, pp. 113–34) notes that they 'have tried to restrain their wages and, occasionally, prices either through a government-coordinated incomes policy (as in the Netherlands and Denmark), or through a centralized system of collective bargaining (as in Sweden and Norway) or through a combination of the two (as in Austria).'

23. As we suggest in Chapter 6, such a situation of stalemate is probably the best characterization of what is happening in Brazil today, as well as in other Latin American countries like Argentina.

24. The administrations of Reagan in the US and Thatcher in the UK are well known for applying this strategy. The success of the policy in terms of the trade-off between inflation and unemployment strongly suggests that the degree of pluralism may be an important factor. Indeed, the US is known for its pluralist features, whereas the UK has many of the traces of Hybrid II systems.

25. Some economists have noted that where there is a clear segmentation in the labour market between 'insiders' (unionized senior employed workers) and 'outsiders' (non-unionized young unemployed workers), and wage bargains take only the former group's interests into account, the trade-off becomes even more stringent. See Blanchard and Summers (1986).

26. Tarantelli is probably the only economist who recognizes Japan as a corporatist case due to the high levels of synchronization of wage bargains and informal centralized bargaining, and the importance of pattern setters. He notes that in Japan 'bargaining takes place mainly at plant level, but it is heavily and yearly coordinated during the so-called spring offensive by all three major trade unions and the government. There is, in addition, a high degree of pattern bargaining' (1987, p. 97).

6. The Institutional Basis of Wage Bargaining in Brazil

Introduction

Much has been written on the conditions of wage restraint, the macroeconomic consequences of unions' activities, and the diversity in the actual behaviour of unions in the advanced countries. But very little on the role of industrial relations in Third World countries. There might be different causes for this lack of interest in the subject.

One may simply be that unions in the South lack the minimum bargaining power to call the attention of researchers to their importance. This is certainly not the case in Latin America where unions' mobilization has been an important element in the political and economic history of the region. Another reason may be that political repression or state corporatism have been effective in controlling labour militancy and turned it into an unimportant factor in explaining macroeconomic phenomena. Finally, because in the 1970s and 1980s real wages carried the burden of adjustment, and workers came to be seen as the victims of the crisis, nobody really thought of unions as active agents in aggravating the crisis.

In countries like Argentina, Uruguay, Chile, Brazil and others in Latin America, where unions played an important political role before the authoritarian wave of the 1960s and 1970s, the macroeconomic effects of the attitudes of workers and unions seem to be far from insignificant. It is the objective of this chapter to study the evolution of the union movement and the collective bargaining structure in Brazil, and their potential connections with the recent stabilization crisis.

We start with the origins of the Brazilian corporatist labour system, and then direct our attention to new developments such as the centralization of the union movement during the 1980s, its relation with political parties, and new trends in collective bargaining. We then look at the effectiveness of policy instruments in recent stabilization attempts, and finally discuss the prospects of a concerted incomes policy.

The Relation Between the State and the Labour Movement

In the following sections we discuss the Brazilian labour system, its origins and late developments, and try to characterize it in terms of the conditions for wage moderation discussed in the previous chapters. We first look at the relation between the State and the development of the labour movement in Brazil between the early 1940s and the early 1990s. The period is divided into three sub-periods corresponding to three broadly defined phases in the political history of the country. The first, from the early 1940s up until the Coup d'Etat of 1964, is characterized by an 'institutionalized state corporatist' system in which the State is able to create an environment of harmonious but increasingly conflictual relation with the unions. The second period, of military rule (1964–77), is marked by a 'repressive corporatist' system in which the control over the labour movement is exercised with the use of force. In the third period, from 1978 to today, in a response to the dependency of the union movement in relation to the State, the re-emergence of union militancy is characterized by high levels of industrial conflict in a system which is best described by the growing 'autonomy and centralization of the labour movement'.

Institutional State Corporatism: Dependency and Avoidance of Conflict

The origin of state corporatism in Brazil is associated with two different but interrelated aspects of the process of late industrialization. The first is a strong presence of the State in shaping the strategy, raising the necessary financial resources and providing the infrastructure for industrial development. The second, as noted by Souza (1978), is the rise of organized labour and socialist parties. In Brazil, both instances were intimately related, and associated with the institutional structure established during the Vargas dictatorship (1937–45).

The State, seen as the strategist and organizer of the process of economic modernization, establishes instruments to 'regulate industrial conflict by incorporating organized labour into an arbitration and bargaining system ... , by using welfare policy and social insurance as tools of social and political control, or, where these measures proved insufficient to secure working class compliance, by the suppression of autonomous labour organizations and their supersession by organs of state control' (Souza, p. 63).[1] The anarchist movements of the beginning of the century in São Paulo seem to have generated enough worries in the dominant classes to lead to the adoption of a detailed labour code which established strong dependency links between the union movement and the State, and which for three decades, served (with decreasing efficacy) the purpose of avoiding major spurs of industrial conflict. The most important dependency ties were the right of the Ministry of Labour to approve the creation of unions, to intervene in unions when their actions were seen as irregular or against the orientation of the Ministry, and to veto the eligibility of certain workers to official posts.

However important institutions may be binding (or more generally, influencing) the actual evolution of potentially conflictual relations, the fact of the matter is that agents need incentives to comply with regulations and the law. In the case of the state corporatist system in Brazil, the incentives to workers were associated with the set of rights which protected them from undue exploitation by employers such as job security, welfare benefits provided by the State and the unions, and the minimum wage. On the part of the leaders, the incentives were representational monopoly and the participation in consulting and decision-making organs of the state, including the labour judicial system. The incentives can be seen as preemptive actions on the part of the State, that is an anticipation of unions' demands and an instrument to avoid, or dampen, the conflict of interests between workers and employers.[2]

The institutional constraints and incentives served their purposes with decreasing effectiveness, especially in the late 1950s and early 1960s when the level of industrial conflict increased dramatically. Indeed, the notion of social chaos, which was clearly associated with, and seen as an important cause of, the Coup d'Etat of 1964 was impregnated with labour disputes, some with political colours. The military saw in the labour movement a focus of communist ideology, and in the attitude of workers an attempt to destabilize the political order.

124

Repressive State Corporatism

The military regime introduced a very small number of changes in the labour code. Indeed, compliance with the existing set of regulations was almost all that was needed. Apart from political repression of resilient union leaders – which should not to be neglected as an important factor in damping the opposition to the new regime – formally, the only two important changes were the new strike law and the adoption of wage controls.

The new regulation of strike activities was quite restrictive making it almost impossible for a union to call a 'legal strike'.[3] If it was declared illegal, the strike had to be immediately suspended. As noted by Sandoval (1984, p. 18),

> the various moments in which the intervention of the labour courts [could] be solicited [by employers] before a strike erupt[ed] mean[t] that the courts [had] the power to decide which strikes [would] be tolerated. In this respect, conflicts over wages and work conditions [were] generally settled by court decisions before a strike [occurred].

The level of strike activity fell dramatically between 1964 and 1977. Not only because the strike rights were restrictive, but also because wage disputes (which accounted for the majority of disputes before 1964) were virtually non-existent in the face of the binding wage controls enforced by the labour justice. Since 1965 the government fixed the annual rate of wage adjustment, thus reducing the scope for wage disputes and, indeed, the discretionary role of the labour courts. The military period was marked by the absence of direct negotiations between unions and employers, and purely bureaucratic activities on the part of labour courts. The combination of the strike law and wage controls created a void in the collective bargaining process.[4]

'New-unionism': Autonomy and Centralization

The new union movement in Brazil is a response to the economic and political model of the 1960s and 1970s in which organized labour and sectors of the middle class were clearly marginalized. The key words here are inequality in the distribution of economic growth and political repression. The process of democratization which started with the Geisel administration in 1974 created an environment in which the re-emergence of the union movement was possible – which does not imply that there were not setbacks or that the opposition to the new movement was not extremely strong. In fact, the demands for union autonomy from the State and the right to negotiate with employers without the interference of the labour justice were not new, having started in the early 1970s (see Souza, 1978, p. 18), but the political climate then was not at all favourable.

The first strikes in 1978 were essentially motivated by economic demands by workers in São Paulo. At that time, the relation between the new union movement and political parties was openly rejected by the union leaders. However, as the movement gained momentum, it very quickly acquired political colours. On the one hand, the new leaders demanded greater autonomy and independence for the union movement in relation to the State. On the other hand, union leaders rapidly became important political actors in a broader movement in favour of redistributive economic measures, an increase in social spending and democratization.

The most characteristic features of the new union movement, and indeed innovative ones in terms of the Brazilian experience, are the search for a centralized structure and its relation with the State. We have in mind the most combative and articulate group of the labour movement which in 1983 created the *Central Única dos Trabalhadores* (CUT).[5]

The incentives for union centralization are far from unambiguous.[6] Unions – and especially the most organized and powerful ones – have obvious incentives to keep their independence in relation to, and not be subject to, a centralized structure. The incentives are even stronger when sectoral-specific interests divide workers. Hence, as noted by Wallerstein (1987, p. 21),

> a decentralized confederal structure allows the affiliated unions to shift back and forth between alliances with their employers and alliances with other unions depending on the policy. In contrast, a centralized confederal structure binds unions in a class coalition and makes more difficult the pursuit of sectoral policies in which the interests of workers of different industries do not coincide. ... The cost of centralization ... depends on the attractiveness of alliances along industrial lines to obtain industry-specific policies.

Industry-specific factors certainly play a role in the attitudes of unions in all economies. Also, in sectors in which the oligopoly power of firms is large, workers usually share the market rents with the firms, and do not have incentives to align with weaker unions. However, the importance of these factors has to be weighted against factors which affect workers in general. Class-based considerations may be more important than sectoral-based factors in different economies, or at different points in time in a given economy. Wallerstein (1987) argues that where all sectors are equally dependent on foreign markets there are strong incentives for union centralization. Indeed, if all unions support export-orientation and free trade they have less cause to guard their capacity for autonomous action. In a sense, the argument holds in the case of Brazil, not because all sectors are equally dependent on external trade, but because they are all highly protected against foreign competition. Indeed, in Brazil, industry-specific factors are not (or have not been) really a concern of union leaders.

However, the most important centripetal forces accounting for the centralization of the union movement in the last ten years in Brazil are ideological, political and institutional in nature. That is, the class-based political incentives to create a strong labour and middle-class coalition seem to be the driving force. Several elements account for this. The military regime had a clear anti-labour bias, and excluded workers from the sharing out of economic gains. It also had a clear anti-left bias which marginalized important sectors of the middle class from political participation. Finally, as a result of the 'investment-oriented strategy' of the 1970s, it had an anti-social bias, which led important groups of the Catholic church who took the side of the poor and marginalized groups through the *Comunidades Eclesiais de Base* in the rural suburban areas, to be politically repressed. These groups (industrial workers, educated middle-class, and the '*descamisados*' through the influence of the church) form the basis of CUT, CGT and CONTAG. What brought them together in the first place was the resistance against the military regime.

Political cleavages within CUT – the most politicized central union – are not insignificant. Whether the different groups, with different social extractions and different experiences during the military regime, are going to stay together, and for how long, it is difficult to say. However, it is important to note that the cleavages inside the central union are associated with differences in ideological lines and strategies, but not with differences between, say, more narrow interests of highly organized industrial unions or industry-specific demands, on the one hand, and the broader interests of the working class as a whole on the other hand. The top priorities of the central union are class-based and horizontal in character rather than group-based demands. The most organized unions, whose leaders have been in CUT since its creation and form the core of the coordination committee, have been defending their own interests in local negotiations since the years of the military regime. The central union, however, has broader demands which apply to workers in general. The rational basis of these demands (agrarian reform under the control of the workers, repudiation of the external and public debts, profit-sharing, increase in social spending) are not always clear and are subject to criticism, but they certainly express a class-based political voice and not the interest of a minority.

There is also an important institutional factor explaining the centralization of the labour movement in recent years. In the face of the history of labour relations in Brazil in which, as noted above, the State and a universal labour code played very important roles, it seems that the most effective way to change labour rights and institutions is through centralized organization and legislative actions. In other words, the lack of a culture of direct negotiations naturally leads to, and at the same time requires, a type of organization which faces the State and the labour code. This organization must have a centralized and horizontal character and its activities must aim at a change in the legislative area.[7]

The political and institutional factors accounting for the centralization of the labour movement reflects an attempt by the union leaders to establish themselves in the 'political market', or to carry their actions beyond the labour market.[8] As noted by Pizzorno (1978, p. 280), differently from collective bargaining, in which the control over the supply of labour and the requirements of 'regularity of work' are the sources of unions' market power, in a situation of political exchange, 'benefits are obtained against the threat to social order or social consensus' and the capacity of unions to destabilize the polity. Indeed, the core issue of the first meetings of union leaders in the early 1980s, and one which really influenced the division of the group between 'moderates' (CGT in the future) and 'radicals' (CUT), was the use of general strikes as weapons against what was seen as employers' and the government intransigence. It seems clear therefore that the motivation behind the centralization of the labour movement in Brazil was the capacity to affect the stability of the polity. Arguments can be made that the centralization of interest organizations may result either in strong destructive conflict and confrontation, or in fruitful cooperation. In the literature on industrial relations one finds convincing theses according to which the incorporation of labour into the established political system tends to reduce labour militancy. Crouch (1985a, pp. 111 and 113), for example, argues that

> once labour has been admitted to the core parties seen to make up the *ministrable* elements of a consociational political system, not only will its representatives cease to seek the overthrow of the capitalist system, but employers will also cease to entertain hopes of a nonunionized labour force. ... The admission of organized labour into political respectability has ... inhibited the two sides of industry from pursuing the massive conflict that characterized systems in earlier periods.

In the Brazilian case, so far, the centralization of the labour movement has strengthened the bargaining power of unions and generated increasingly conflictual attitudes. The extent to which the costs of conflict will lead to an incorporation of labour and generate a more cooperative environment is still very uncertain.

A second characteristic feature of the new union movement is its relation with the State. Independence and autonomy in relation to the corporatist structure (Ministry of Labour and Labour Justice), and strong relationship with the *Partido dos Trabalhadores* (PT) – actually founded before the CUT in 1982 by the same workers' leaders – are the central elements here. Union leaders affiliated with CUT have been clearly against the corporatist structure in which every action of the union is ultimately dependent on the State's acquiescence.

The tendency towards greater centralization of the movement and the demands for autonomy in relation to the State do not imply that the formal structure of the labour organization in Brazil is really that different from what it was in the 1950s. Formally, that is according to the prevailing Labour Code, unions are organized on an industry and regional basis at the local, state (federation) and national (confederation) levels. Until very recently (1988) central unions were banned and there was a compulsory contribution which all workers (unionized or not) have to pay. Hence, state corporatist institutions are still in place, and old union leaders still play an important role. The new leaders entered the official structure in order to remove the old and more conservative leaders, and gradually are trying to modify the formal apparatus.

The extent of the changes is still uncertain. Some of the reminiscences of the corporatist structure (most prominently the union organization based on industrial sectors at the state and national levels) do not seem to be in the agenda for future changes. Hence, the coexistence for some time of a centralized structure with strong sectoral branches is a clear possibility.

The relation with the PT is also an important element in the characterization of the new union movement in Brazil. Historically there seems to exist a strong correlation between the success of labour parties and the centralization of the union movement. Centralized union movements, because of their class-based interests, help labour parties in elections – and this has clearly been the case in Brazil where a significant number of union leaders from CUT have been elected representatives at both the state and federal levels and mayors of important cities, and one, Mr Luis Inacio Lula da Silva, ran for the presidency of the republic and ended second in 1989. In a survey conducted in the third congress of the CUT, 91% of the delegates voted for PT candidates. On the other hand, a strong labour party helps the creation of a bridge between the demands of the central union and the legislative process. In Brazil, these positive feed-back effects have been very important in consolidating both the PT and the CUT. However, as the party attempts to gain a broader base, the relation between the central union and the party becomes increasingly difficult. Indeed, this has been a historical problem for labour and social democratic parties in Europe (see Przeworski, 1985). During the elaboration of the 1988 new Constitution, the CUT made a number of proposals through the PT and other left parties. The proposals had a clear social democratic tone: their main objective was to protect the workers from market fluctuations and to increase their bargaining power in negotiations with employers. The increase in the costs of dismissals, on the one hand, and the right to strike, on the other, are the best examples in this connection. As for more specific labour rights (reduction in work time, increase in annual bonus, and so on), the objective of the CUT was to extend to all workers the achievements of the most organized unions in São Paulo. In most cases, the demands were included in the Constitution, and there is very little doubt that CUT came out of this process as a winner. Although not explicitly mentioned in their programmes or in the discourse of their most prominent leaders, the dominant stream within both the CUT and PT has a clearly social democratic inclination. Indeed, the positions and strategies followed by the central union and the party, and the relation between the two, resemble those of the European central unions and social democratic parties in the inter-war period and after the Second World War.[9] Rodrigues (1990), an expert on the history of the union movement in Brazil, notes that:

> it is clear that within the majority group [in the central union] there are strong forces pushing in the direction of a social-democratic line, which would tend to direct the CUT to the attainment of economic gains and social and political reforms within the market economy.

Inside the central union there are disputes over the objectives and strategies to be followed. To be sure, there are groups who firmly oppose an acceptance of capitalist rules of the game, and see the socialist revolution as an aim. During the preparation of the new Constitution these groups were against the idea of using the established institutional apparatus to voice demands. Instead, a 'general strike' was advocated. The revolutionary groups favour a combative strategy, strongly rooted at the firm level, and oppose any political concertation involving employers or the parties of the centre and the right.

The majority of the groups represented in the central union, however, favour negotiations within the prevailing institutional apparatus. Indeed, the president of the CUT has been quite clear in asserting that the central union should not declare itself revolutionary, though some of its members may be revolutionary socialists (see Rodrigues, 1990), The attitudes of the central union's leaders, more than their rhetoric, are a sign of their social democratic preferences. As noted already, these actions have been in the direction of increasing the political power of the unions and forcing the adoption of social reforms which intend to insulate the workers' income from market fluctuations. As noted, the CUT played an important role during the elaboration of the new Constitution and has kept open the possibility of negotiating an incomes policy with the government.

The Social and Political Profile of the New-Union Movement

The CUT was born in 1983, and so far three national congresses have taken place – in 1983 when it was founded, in 1986 and 1989. The majority of the groups represented in the congresses come from the rural sector. This might seem somewhat surprising since the union movement is usually associated with the strikes of the industrial workers of São Paulo in 1978 and 1979. As noted already, however, the growth of the rural movement is clearly a result of the grassroots movement of the Catholic church, especially in the rural areas of the Northeast and North regions of the country. Services comes in second place and industry in third. Over time, public servants had their representation increased from 7% in the first congress to 16% in the third congress. The representations of industrial workers also increased, from 15.4% to 20.1%.

When the data are regionally desegregated (for the third congress), the proportion of industrial delegates from the industrialized Southeast is around 13%. More than half (actually 61%) of the rural delegates come from the less industrialized regions (North, Northeast and Centre West). In terms of the overall regional distribution, the Southeast has a clear majority (35%), but other regions also have a fair representation.

The coordinating board of the central union has 20 members of which seven come from the industrial sector, five from the services sector, two from education, two from the agricultural sector, two from public services, and two from liberal professions. Of the seven coming from the industrial sector, five come from the core of the union movement in São Paulo – the metal workers. Hence, when we look at the composition of the top leadership of the CUT, the representation of industrial workers dominates the others. The chief coordinator, Jair Menegelli, who is also the president of the metal workers' union of São Bernardo do Campo e Diadema, has been in the job since the central union was created. Most of the workers who founded the CUT were not members of the official union structure. Indeed, in the first and second congresses, when the central union was still being organized, the proportion of delegates who were not official union leaders outnumbered the proportion of elected leaders and directors of official unions. In the third congress the number of official union leaders is greater than the number of

Table 6.1 Groups represented in CUT's congresses (by sectors of activity)

	Ind.	Public sector	Rural	Trans-port	Fin.	Ser-vices	Oth.	Total
1st con-gress								
(1984)	144.0	68.0	308.0	0	0	246.0	171.0	937.0
(%)	15.4	7.2	33.0	0	0	26.2	18.2	100.0
2nd con-gress								
(1986)	182.0	114.0	366.0	0	0	276.0	76.0	1014.0
(%)	17.9	11.2	36.1	0	0	27.2	7.6	100.0
3rd con-gress								
(1989)	233.0	185.0	374.0	28.0	48.0	289.0	0	1157.0
(%)	20.1	16.0	32.4	2.4	4.1	25.0	0	100.0

Source: CUT as reported by Rodrigues (1990).

rank-and-file leaders. This change has two important implications. On the one hand it means that CUT leaders have effectively penetrated the official union structure, essentially winning elections.And on the other, that the central union had become more institutionalized and structured. Not only that, but one important decision approved in the third congress was that from then on the representation of each union has to be proportional to the number of affiliated workers in the union.

Collective Bargaining

The periodization used in the discussion on State–labour relations

Table 6.2 Delegates by sector of activity and region (third congress, 1989, % of total of 6218 delegates)

	North	North-east	C.West	South-east	South	To-tal
Rural	6.6	9.8	3.0	6.1	6.7	32.2
Industry	1.4	4.5	0.5	13.8	4.0	24.2
Services	1.4	5.1	3.5	7.1	4.5	21.6
Public sector	1.4	4.7	1.6	5.4	2.6	15.7
Financial	0.1	0.7	0.3	2.0	0.9	4.0
Transport	0.0	0.4	0.2	1.3	0.4	2.3
Total	10.9	25.2	9.1	35.7	19.1	100.0

Source: CUT as reported by Rodrigues (1990)

can also be applied to the analysis of collective bargaining. Until 1964 only half of the labour contracts resulted from direct negotiations between the union and employers. Working conditions and hours of work were based on the labour code, and only demands which exceeded those established in the law were subject to negotiations. In general, disputes over these issues were very rare. Mericle (1974) notes that as inflation accelerated in the late 1950s and early 1960s, wage adjustment became an important, if not the only, issue for negotiation. In fact, most of the strikes in the period were associated with demands for wage increases – strikes over working conditions were rare.

Mericle studied 23 contracts in the state of São Paulo in March of 1964, and concludes that 'none of the contracts resemble the comprehensive agreements which are common in North America. ... [O]f the sample of 23 contracts and court cases, 21 were concerned exclusively with the size and application of the wage increase' (p. 205). As reported in Table 6.4, around 50% of the collective bargains studied by Mericle did not involve the labour justice, and in 25% of the cases, there were judicial arbitrations. After 1964, the combination of the new strike law and the introduction of wage controls reduced dramatically the bargaining power of the unions. Direct negotiations and even judicial agreements became quite rare. In all cases, the labour courts arbitrated in accordance with the government's wage law. In 1970, direct negotiations accounted for only 19% of the cases in a sample of 47 cases studied by Mericle; in 55% of the cases there was judicial arbitration. Employers did not have any incentive to negotiate with the unions: they knew that the labour court would simply follow the wage law, and that unions did not have much of a bargaining power. The usual procedure was to refuse to negotiate with the union, and take the case to the labour court.

As a result of the binding constraint imposed on wage negotiations by the wage law, unions moved into non-wage demands. Mericle (1974, pp. 228–9) notes that in a sample of 35 important unions in the state of São Paulo studied in the period 1964–71, only one did not make any non-wage demand. Demands included reductions in the duration of work, working conditions, and bonuses among others, and a not insignificant proportion of them were won. However, in most cases in which the unions were successful, the negotiation had taken place at the firm level, and the gains were not extended to other workers in the industry.

The greatest differences between the 1980s and the previous periods are the following: (a) direct negotiations between unions and employers became the rule; (b) the wage policy gradually lost its efficacy as a coordinating instrument; (c) non-wage demands gradually spread out; and (d) the central unions (in particular, CUT) started playing an important role in negotiations. In what follows we discuss the changes in the nature of collective bargains over the last ten years.

As seen in Table 6.4, the proportion of direct agreements to judicial agreements in the state of São Paulo jumped from 0.23 in 1970–71 to 2.43 in 1981 and then remained above one in 1982–4; the percentage of judicial arbitrations to the total number of cases went from 55% to 3% in 1982, 11% in 83 and 9% in 1984.

As noted already, the structure of the labour movement in Brazil is in a process of change. The central unions were very active and indeed quite influential in the discussion over minimum standards as far as labour conditions and workers' rights in the new

Table 6.3 Distribution of delegates

	Glassroots delegates	Official union leaders	Total
First congress	3440.0	1782.0	5222.0
(%)	65.9	34.1	100.0
Second congress	3649.0	1532.0	5181.0
(%)	70.4	29.6	100.0
Third congress	3178.0	306.0	6243.0
(%)	50.9	49.1	100.0

Source: CUT as reported by Rodrigues (1990).

Constitution were concerned. In a sense, this can be seen as an indication that part of the collective bargaining process does take place at the national level. To the extent that local bargaining is concerned, the degree of centralization of negotiations varies from sector to sector, and from region to region. Pastore and Zylberstajn (1988, p. 63) have carefully studied the recent patterns of bargaining, and concluded that both the CUT and CGT have been looking for

> negotiations of minimum standards at the federation level and freedom to negotiate additional clauses at the level of the firm. Innumerable agreements signed at the level of the federation [between 1984 and 1986] had to be altered ... in order to provide better conditions to workers at the level of the firm. As a general trend, we move towards a conception of negotiation akin to the European system in which there are centralized negotiations (at the federation level) over minimum standards, and decentralized mechanisms (at the level of the firm).

Indeed, it has become a common procedure to have negotiations starting at a very high level of aggregation in the industry (to define the minimum standards), and as the demands become more specific (or simply prohibitive for the smaller firms), to have negotiations at lower levels. In some cases the central union (CUT especially) plays an important role in providing professional negotiators who bargain in the name of the local unions at high levels of aggregation in the industry. Furthermore in some important sectors, with powerful unions (banking and oil refineries being the best examples here), negotiations take place at the national level with obvious spill-over and demonstration effects. The role of the central unions in collective bargaining and through the extension of bargaining achievements to the legislative area has been to elevate the standards of the less organized groups. On the other hand, it is indisputable that the stronger unions have also profited from the political power of the central organizations to improve (beyond the minimum standards) the conditions of their members. However, these unions would do better than those less organized anyway, which leads to the conclusion that the central unions have played an important part in reducing the disparities and inequalities.[10]

It is difficult to anticipate what is going to be the typical pattern of negotiations in the future – if there will be in fact a typical pattern. Be that as it might, there are certain trends worth nothing.The CUT have been proposing a centralized national collective bargain followed by localized negotiations.

It is not clear if the central union would favour second-layer negotiations at the sectoral level or the level of the firm. Employers' associations are clearly against the proposal for they fear that centralized bargaining would enhance to an undue measure the central union's bargaining power. Their experience with the new Constitution was an indication in this respect: the unions were well organized and had very clear demands whereas the employers' associations kept a very defensive position.

The National Confederation of Industry (CNI) – the employers' association – has strengthened its department of industrial relations in recent years, and its central activity has been to put together sectoral conferences of human resources specialists with the aim of establishing negotiation standards. This seems to be a strong indication that the CNI is anticipating a greater centralization of negotiations at the sectoral/national level.

In the face of current trends, it seems quite unlikely that the system will converge towards a totally decentralized system. The most probable scenario seems to be a consolidation of the current state, in which local bargains at the level of the firm will continue

Table 6.4 Nature of collective bargaining – São Paulo, 1964–1984

	Direct Agreement / Judicial agreement or arbitrat. (ratio)	Direct Agreement/ Total (%)	Judicial Agreement/ Total (%)	Judicial Arbitrat/ Total (%)
1964 (March)	0.92	48	26	26
1970–71	0.23	19	26	55
1979	0.63	--	--	--
1980	0.96	--	--	--
1981	2.43	--	--	--
1982	1.88	66	31	3
1983	1.11	53	37	11
1984	1.20	54	36	9

Calculations by the author. *Source of data*: Mericle (1964 and 1970–1), Vasconcelos (1979–81), and Aguirre et al. (1982–4).

to be the last layer of negotiations while minimum standards will be negotiated at the industry, and possibly national, level. The characteristics of the Brazilian system clearly put it among those classified in the second section of Chapter 5 as 'hybrid' systems. It has elements of the Polar I system (increasing centralization of unions' organization and participation of confederations in collective bargains) and of the Polar II system (decentralized negotiations). However, it is much closer to the Hybrid II case than to the Hybrid I case. Indeed, the negotiations of minimum standards take place at the industry level and the level of synchronization of negotiations is extremely low. Moreover, the relation between the government and the unions has been quite disastrous (as noted below). All these factors account for a complete lack of macroeconomic coordination in the formation of wages and prices, and hence do not contribute to wage restraint.

Trade Independence and Accommodative Policies

There are some aspects of the Brazilian experience which account for a lack of solid restrictions on wage and price increases. Not only is the degree of industrial concentration very high in many industrial sectors – thus providing firms with great market powers – but, in general, the economy is very closed and protected from foreign competition. The import substitution strategy is obviously responsible for the lack of external competition. Since the 1950s, a deliberate policy to protect domestic industries has been systematically implemented.

Because import substitution and protection have become part of the Brazilian culture, and indeed can be seen as one of the most stable rules of the game in the country, managers did not have to even worry about the prospects of eventually facing international competition. The protection against foreign competition also resulted from the exchange rate policy adopted since the late 1960s which indexed the exchange rate to inflation, thus providing an insurance against price increases. Subsidies to export sectors completes the list of instruments used to insulate the industrial sector.

Accommodative monetary and fiscal policies also reduce the constraints to wage and price inflation. Economic growth and the creation of employment posts have been for a long time an important shield against opposition and social unrest used by (both military and civilian) governments in Brazil. It is quite true that in 1981–3 a policy-driven recession interrupted more than ten years of accelerated growth. But this was an isolated episode, and understandably so in a country in which a significant share of the labour force lives in urban areas and in which safety nets (unemployment benefits most notably) did not exist until 1986. From 1984 until the beginning of the Collor administration in 1990, with the consolidation of the democratic regime, and the growth of the union movement, the word 'recession' was banned from the official vocabulary of both the right and left, thus reducing any serious threats of unemployment.

Dissatisfaction, Instability and Government Credibility

As noted above, since 1964 a wage law establishes the adjustment parameter of wages to past inflation and the indexation period, that is the time span between adjustments. In principle, the policy applies to all wages in the economy. The wage policy can be seen as a non-negotiated incomes policy explicitly conceived as an instrument to prevent wages from creating inflationary pressures. As described by the architect of the first version of the law, it was meant to replace strikes, pressures and distributive conflicts by a simple arithmetic calculation (see Simonsen, 1983).

Wage controls were quite effective between 1964 and 1978–9, and played an important role not only in stabilizing the economy, but also in bringing down the rate of inflation as wages were systematically underindexed to past inflation in the first ten years.[11] The effectiveness of the law resulted in a large measure from the repressive character of the regime. Not even the labour justice which in the 1950s and 1960s had the right to arbitrate wage disputes could deviate from the wage law. Indeed, as noted by Mericle, writing in 1974,

> Wage increases are ... calculated by applying a ... formula to data supplied by the government. The courts are required by law to use both the formula and the data in the arbitration decisions which they render. Furthermore, all cases in which the parties reach agreement without court intervention must be registered with the labour courts, where the increase is promptly appealed if it exceeds the government index. Voluntary agreements in excess of the formula figure are always overturned in the Supreme Labour Court. Thus, the size of all ... wage increases is, in effect, centrally controlled. (Mericle, p. 264)

The law was altered in 1968 and 1975 with the introduction of an *ex post* corrective factor to account for reductions in the wage due to the possible underestimation of inflation, and to shorten from 24 to 12 months the reference period of the average purchasing power of wages which the rule was supposed to restore. These changes can be seen as a response to the many criticisms that the wage law was responsible for the deterioration of the distribution of income during the 1960s.

With the acceleration of inflation in the second half of the 1970s and the re-emergence of strike activities in 1978, two new elements start affecting the dynamics of wage (and price) formation. The first is the reduction of the official adjustment period from one year until 1979 to six months thereafter. The different policies adopted together with the so-called 'heterodox shocks' between 1986 and 1989 had even shorter adjustment periods. The second, and more important new element, is the return of direct negotiations between unions and employers, and of the right of the labour courts to validate or arbitrate wage adjustments which incorporated real wage gains associated with increases in 'productivity'. This opened a door for wage adjustments above the past rate of inflation. Another important instrument to protect wages against the acceleration of inflation was the demand by unions of reductions in the adjustment period of wages, independently of the period fixed by the wage law.

Both the reduction of the indexation period and the 'overindexation' of wages in respect to past inflation imply increase in real wages if the rate of inflation remains the same.[12] However, in the face of the degree of protection of the Brazilian industry, and the level of oligopoly power of firms in many sectors of the economy, firms were able to protect their profit margin by indexing (or overindexing) changes in costs. The race between wages and prices seems to be an important element of the acceleration of inflation during the 1980s.

At this point it is important to consider two policy-related elements which accounted for the increasing degree of distributive conflict and explosive trajectory of inflation in Brazil. One is the adjustment to the debt crisis in the late 1970s and early 1980s through currency devaluations with obvious inflationary pressures. Were the unions impotent to respond to the acceleration of inflation, the reductions in real wages would have been dramatic. Actually, the average real wage (and especially the average product wage) fell considerably in 1983–4 but in many sectors unions were able to resist the shock. In fact, relative wages changed considerably during this period.[13]

The second policy-related aspect which deserves notice is the series of heterodox shocks applied to the economy after 1986. These shocks were exacerbations of the wage (and price) control policies of the previous period with the difference that the union movement now had greater bargaining power, and firms did not have less market power than before. Price freezes and tight wage controls are hardly effective in an environment of rapidly changing relative prices, workers' dissatisfaction, and distributive conflict. A non-negotiated incomes policy in a system in which agents have considerable market power and can effectively defy the government's measures is doomed to be rendered ineffective. This is not meant to be a simplistic criticism of the policies, nor to imply that there are easy alternatives, but only to point out the structural and institutional obstacles.

Policy failures – either due to an inept reading of the conjuncture by the government, or to inconsistent goals – are not as important to us as their consequences for the behaviour of the actors (unions in particular). Since 1979 a series of policies aimed at adjusting the economy to the debt crisis, and coping with an accelerating rate of inflation, resulted in growing instability and loss of credibility of the government. The recurrence of unexpected inflationary and policy shocks, and resulting fluctuations in real wages tend to create an extremely defensive attitude on the part of workers and unions which is reflected in attempts to protect real wages against shocks through the overindexation of money wages and reductions of the indexation period.

A measure of workers' dissatisfaction and distributive conflict is the level of strike activity. In what follows we present some figures on strike activities in the Brazilian economy. Table 6.5 compiles information from three different sources. The data for the period 1955–80, borrowed from Sandoval (1984), clearly shows that after a positive trend in the late 1950s and early 1960s, there is a substantial reduction in the number of strikes after 1964, and a strong resurgence in 1978–80. Between 1981 and 1984 – years of negative industrial growth – the number of strikes as reported by Tavares de Almeida (1988) grew from 144 to 492. Between 1986 and 1989 the number of strikes reported by the Secretary of Labour went from 843 to 3164.

During the 1980s, all the ingredients against wage restraint seemed to be present in Brazil. Not only institutional and structural factors – hybrid/intermediary type of collective bargaining and trade independence – but also conjunctural factors (lack of credibility of the government and growing instability) account for the defensive behaviour of unions with obvious effects on the aggravation of the crisis.

142

Wage Policy Ineffectiveness and Overindexation

There is evidence of a gradual loss of effectiveness of the wage policy and of overindexation of wages during the 1980s in Brazil. Before we turn to the evidence, it is important to note that the lack of wage restraint is not inflationary by itself. The impact on inflation depends on the pricing behaviour of firms. If firms mark up costs then overindexation is clearly inflationary. The extent to which firms are willing, or are forced, to assimilate changes in costs by reducing their profit margins determines the effect of wage variations on the rate of inflation.

The first evidence of overindexation is provided in Table 6.5. The table shows increases in real wages (demanded and by unions and actual) due to 'productivity gains'. The years 1982–4 were marked by a very strong recession, and quite clearly productivity increased much less than real wages in the period which obviously is characterized by the presence of overindexation.[14]

Further evidence of the ineffectiveness of wage controls in the

Table 6.5 Strikes in Brazil, 1955–80

1955–56	18	1982	144
1957–58	53	1983	347
1959–60	132	1984	492
1963–64	215	1985	843
1965–66	30	1986	1493
1967–68	22	1987	2275
1971–72	192	1988	1914
1978–80	338	1989	3164
1981	150		

Sources: 1955–80 (Sandoval, 1984, 29), 1981–84 (NEPP, UNICAMP, as reported by Tavares de Almeida), and 1985–89 (Ministério do Trabalho, Brazil).

1980s, or the presence of overindexation, is provided in aneconometric work by Camargo (1990). He shows that both the conditions of the labour market (as measured by the rate of unemployment) and the degree of dissatisfaction of workers (as measured by the ratio of the institutional wage to a proxy of the 'target wage'[15]) affect the determination of the 'wage drift', or the difference between the institutional wage and the actual wage. In particular, the greater the rate of unemployment and the lower the degree of dissatisfaction of workers, the greater the adherence of the actual wage to the institutional wage.

Marinho (1990), also in an econometric work, shows that real wages in the oligopolist sectors of the Brazilian industry tend to grow as inflation accelerates, the opposite occurring with wages in the more competitive sector. This is not necessarily an evidence that money wages in the oligopolist sectors are the primary causes of the acceleration of inflation. It may simply be an indication that as a response to the acceleration of inflation (due to other causes), unions in the oligopolist sectors are able to increase money wages ahead of past and current inflation, thus creating additional inflationary pressures. If unions in other sectors cannot overindex their wages, there is a tendency for real wages in the oligopolist sectors to increase.

The clearest evidence of overindexation in the Brazilian experience, as shown in detail in the following chapter, is given by the ratio between annual variations of money wages in industry and CPI inflation between 1976 and 1990. The ratio turns out to begreater than 1 over the period, with the exception of a few months during the 1981-3 recession. In another study (Amadeo, 1991a), it is shown that the estimated mark-up of firms remained approximately constant over the period. Taking the levels of indexation of wages (with respect to CPI inflation) and industrial prices (with respect to changes in costs) together, it becomes obvious that strong inflationary pressures were created in the industrial sector.

Stabilization and Concerted Incomes Policy

During the 1980s, the coordinating capability of the Brazilian government has been gradually reduced. The rapid acceleration of inflation over the decade can be seen as the result of a distributive conflict involving the government, firms and workers.

Table 6.6 Average increase in real wage due to 'productivity gains' (% of wage after adjustment for inflation, annual average, industry)

	Direct agreements		Judicial agreement or decision	
	Demanded	Actual	Demanded	Actual
1982				
São Paulo	12.8	3.9	12.8	5.3
Rio de Janeiro	13.0	3.2	10.3	4.6
Minas Gerais	8.2	3.3	9.4	4.4
1983				
São Paulo	11.4	3.9	12.6	5.3
Rio de Janeiro	**	**	7.6	3.9
Minas Gerais	6.7	2.3	8.1	4.7
1984				
São Paulo	13.3	**	9.8	7.0
Rio de Janeiro	**	**	7.8	4.4
Minas Gerais	9.5	**	8.6	**

Source: Aguirre et al., 1985. Obs.: the data for 1984 refer to the first semester only. (**) Data not available.

The government participates in this conflict in two different, but interrelated, instances. On the one hand, in trying to adjust the economy to the external debt crisis, two major devaluations of the domestic currency intended to change relative prices in favour of tradable goods created obvious inflationary pressures. On the other hand, given the interrelation between the rate of inflation and the government deficit (due to the indexation of public bonds), the Treasury and the Central Bank have had to recurrently finance the debt by either issuing new debt or increasing the supply of money, thus reducing the government's flexibility in conducting monetary and fiscal policies.

Agents in the private sector, in turn, respond to supply shocks and rising uncertainty over the path of future inflation by trying to protect their income through overindexation. We have already noted the reduction in the degree of effectiveness of wage controls. The loss of control over macroeconomic variables led the government in March 1986 (and again in June 1987, January 1989, March 1990 and February 1991) to adopt so-called 'heterodox stabilization programmes' based on wage and price controls. However, in a system in which there is a lack of credibility in the government's ability to impose costs on free-riders, and with a significant number of 'large' free-riders (that is, agents with considerable market power), the coordinating power of wage and price controls becomes negligible.

The use of market instruments (fiscal and particularly monetary policies) to support the incomes policy was seen as unnecessary in 1986 because of the level of popular acquiescence surrounding the government's programme. The actual level of acquiescence turned out to be much smaller as time went by, and the large free-riders started boycotting the programme. In the other two plans of the Sarney government, market solutions were not implemented on account of the absolute lack of political support of the government.

The experience so far has demonstrated that non-negotiated incomes policies (wage and price controls) are quite ineffective, and the market approach too costly (and also rather ineffective) in the Brazilian case. The institutional apparatus on which wages are negotiated (decentralized and dis-synchronized bargaining), the structural features of the economy (highly protected industry in particular), and the growing uncertainty concerning the eventuality of future policy shocks, seem to be at the root of the stabilization crisis and the inability of the government to coordinate the economy.

Over the decade many attempts to establish a 'social pact', or a concerted incomes policy, have taken place. The government, in the face of a deterioration of the situation, would appeal to the organized agents (employers' and workers' associations), and try to engage in a national agreement. None of the attempts had a real prospect of success. Institutional, political and economic factors explain why the attempts were, from the very beginning, doomed to failure. As already noted, the degree of centralization of the union movement has been growing significantly over time, and this should be seen as a positive sign. But on the other hand, there are political cleavages within the major confederation (CUT) and between confederations which do impose certain difficulties for an agreement. On the employers' side, the problem of representation is even more serious which implies that if an agreement was to be in fact signed, the level of compliance to the guidelines would probably be very low. Furthermore, there is a complete lack of experience in negotiating at the national level, and none of the parties involved, including the government, have a solid conception of the means and goals associated with a concerted programme.

As for the political conditions, the exclusion of organized labour from the political arena for so many years during the military regime has led union leaders to be very sceptical about agreements with employers and the government. It is true that a strong relation exists between the union movement and the political parties. But on the other hand, union leaders do not hold any key positions in government agencies, and hence do not have effective political power within the administration. Indeed, during the 1980s, the unions saw themselves as outsiders, and accordingly, as far as their relation with the government was concerned, had a very independent and combative attitude. However, it cannot be said that the union movement has had an irresponsible attitude. In fact, it has been willing to engage in negotiations but has not yet seen any evidence that workers will become co-responsible for the management of certain key instruments in the economy. It seems legitimate to argue that neither the government nor the employers are prepared to share with the unions the power over the process of production (at the firm level) and the management of the economy (at the national level).

The distributive conflict between workers and firms seems to be at the heart of the high levels of industrial confrontation of the past years. Unions and employers have quite dissonant perspectives as to what is fair and what is feasible as far as the distribution of income is concerned. As a result of differences in perspectives the level of disputes has been growing, and also the level of uncertainty and instability. The lack of a range of consensual economic outcomes implies that agents are very often dissatisfied with their conditions.

There is a shortage of consensual long-run goals and an excess of self-protection based on very short-run foresights. The demands do not add up to one, and macroeconomic imbalances ensue. The government intervenes with strong measures, but is too weak to make them effective. A sense of chaos and disorder grows in the economy, information becomes very cacophonous, the agents feel insecure and rational behaviour brings about inconsistent macroeconomic outcomes.

Two views of the future are possible. One is that the growing levels of conflict and instability will lead organized agents to conclude eventually that the cooperative solution is superior to the individualistic approach. In this sense, the greater the level of centralization and organization of interests around a few key associations and, paradoxically enough, the greater the degree of conflict, the greater becomes the likelihood of a cooperative solution. The pessimist view is that entropic forces are very strong, that agents have myopic perspectives, and will never seek the cooperative approach.

Notes

1. The adoption of corporatist institutions in Brazil is usually associated with the Fascist regime in Italy but, in fact, as noted by Esping-Andersen and Korpi (1985, pp. 180–81), corporatist relations were introduced much earlier in other European countries:

   In nations such as Germany and Austria where capitalism became established under neo-absolutist, statist auspices, an active social policy had emerged [before the First World War]. It was explicitly designed to preserve stability and arrest socialism by granting rights independent of market participation. Social reform pursued a corporatist, status-segregated order designed to reward loyalty and traditional privilege, and to discourage wage-earner unification.

2. Collier and Collier (1979) have analysed the evolution of industrial relation in some Latin American countries in terms of State/unions relations characterized by different doses of 'inducements' (incentives) and 'constraints' (institutional constraints) over time.

3. Mericle (1974, p. 202) provides a synthesis of the strike law imposed by the military government:

   strikes are legal in two situations: in interest disputes over the negotiation of new contracts, and in disputes over the enforcement of the wage clauses of a court decision or collective contract. The enforcement strikes can only occur if the employer is behind in wage payments or if he fails to pay the specified wage rate. Other contract enforcement disputes are subject to the grievance procedure of the conciliation courts. Strikes during the life of a contract or court decision are illegal if their objective is to alter the terms of the contract. Political and solidarity strikes are also illegal.

4. Sandoval (1984, p. 20) notes that 'by greatly restricting legal strike actions and by withdrawing salary and working condition questions from the arena of collective negotiation, the government sought to perfect the autocratic structure and eliminate class conflict, while the unions retained only the task of administrating their welfare activities.'

5. The other group was essentially composed of members of the official movement during the military period, and had a more conservative perspective. In 1983 the two groups broke away: one created the CUT and the other kept its original name (CONCLAT) and in 1986 became the *Central Geral dos Trabalhadores* (CGT). Our analysis applies almost exclusively to the CUT which at the same time is clearly numerically dominant and represents the innovative element in the Brazilian labour movement.

6. We mean by 'centralization' a tendency towards an institutional centralization of the union movement around two major central unions (CUT and CGT) and one rural central union (CONTAG). This tendency does not imply the non-existence of important political cleavages between confederations and within confederations (and we shall refer to them presently – most notably those within CUT).

7. Whereas in Western countries the centralization of the union (and employers') movements is seen as positive in the face of the obvious ties between centralization and the sensitiveness of collective actors to policies – thus enhancing coordination – in Brazil both the government and employers show signs of circumspection in respect to the issue for they associate centralization with the growth of the political power of unions.

8. Korpi and Shalev (1979, p. 170; cited by Cameron, 1985, p. 146) argue that 'to the extent that labour is successful in acquiring control over political institutions, it can exercise its power through these means and will not be limited to the industrial arena.'

9. The attempts to increase job security and expand the coverage of unemployment benefits can be seen as an effort to 'decommodify labour' to use Esping-Andersen and Korpi's term. This author notes that

> social democratic class formation ... is first and foremost a struggle to decommodify labour and stem market sovereignty in order to make collective action possible. Only when workers command resources and access to welfare independently of market exchange can they possibly be swayed not to take jobs during strike actions, underbid fellow workers, and so forth. (1985, p. 31)

Esping-Andersen also refers to the centralization of the union movement and the relation with the political system as a typical social democratic strategy:

> In respect of the movement, social democracy depends on the 'nationalization' and centralized coordination of trade unionism and on optimal electoral penetration by the party. The first precondition is the victory of vertically organized and nationally centralized trade unionism. ... Trade union centralization is also necessary for coherence between the union movement and the political party. (p. 33)

10. In comparative analyses of advanced OECD countries, it has been found that where the degree of centralization of the union movement is greater and its role in collective bargaining more important, pay differentials are smaller. See Treu (1987).

11. Between 1964 and 1968 the formula used to adjust wages had a term which depended on the expected rate of inflation. The latter systematically underestimated the actual rate of inflation thus implying a reduction in the real wage. It has been estimated that between

1964 and 1967 the real wage in the industry fell 9.1%.

12. See Lopes (1986), Ros (1989) and Amadeo (1991).

13. See Amadeo (1991a).

14. We are not arguing that the increase in real wages was not fair but only that money wages in those years grew faster than past inflation.

15. The institutional wage is defined as the wage as determined by the wage policy; and the target wage is assumed to be equal to the real wage obtained in the last negotiation.

7. Macroeconomic Crisis, the Labour Market and Distribution in Brazil

Introduction

The macroeconomic performance of the Brazilian economy and its consequences for the behaviour of the labour market and the distribution of income during the late 1970s and the 1980s are strongly affected by interrelated factors which, in principle, also have dynamics of their own. On the one hand, we have the restrictions imposed on the policy alternatives by the oil shocks in the 1970s and the interest rate shock of the early 1980s. Such restrictions implied a greater stringency of the trade-offs between the solutions for external and domestic macroeconomic goals and between the fiscal balance and stabilization attempts. On the other hand, we have changes in the bargaining power of important sectors of society, with significant consequences for the distribution of income and the movement of relative wages.

However successful the external adjustment has been in Brazil, important negative sequels developed in the late 1980s. Prominent among these is the significant reduction in the capacity of the government to continue investing in infrastructure and expanding the provision of social goods on account of the relation between the external debt and the domestic fiscal deficit. Another sequel is the acceleration of inflation which resulted from devaluations of the domestic currency (cruzeiro) in 1979 and again in 1983, the gradual advancement of indexation schemes and the 'new inflation' associated with a sequence of unsuccessful 'heterodox' stabilization programmes. During the 1980s the deterioration of the fiscal situation and the increase in the volatility of inflation gave rise to growing uncertainty and, as a consequence, the stagnation of the economic activity.

The capacity of the government to re-establish the fiscal balance, reduce inflation and recover 'animal spirits' has declined continuously since the mid-1980s. The series of unsuccessful heterodox stabilization programmes based on price freezes led to a gradual reduction in the coordinating capability of the government.

The clientelistic nature of the State in Brazil has also contributed to a decline in the credibility of the government giving rise to an intensification of the derangement of the social relations. These factors together explain the difficulties in establishing an agenda for freeing the country from the stagnation trap of the last ten years.

The democratization process inaugurated in the late 1970s led, as expected, to a spectacular spread of redistributive demands – in particular on the part of the most organized labour groups which, as a result of the political repression, had remained silent during the military regime. The distribution conflict between capital and organized labour became clearly more intense during the 1980s with significant effects on the path of inflation and the outcome of stabilization attempts. Industrial relations were also affected by the appearance and development of the so-called new unionism movement as discussed in Chapter 6, with extraordinary consequences for the workers' rights. These factors have had important impacts on the conditions and responses of the labour market and on the redistribution of the wage bill among the labour groups as a result of differences in their relative bargaining power.

This chapter deals with the multiple dimensions of the economic crisis which gradually assaulted the Brazilian economy during the 1980s, namely, the attempts to adjust the economy to changes in the environment and constraints, the effects on the labour market and the distribution of income – most notably the movement in relative wages. Accordingly, the chapter is divided into three parts. The first part discusses the macroeconomic environment and the efforts to promote the' adjustment to the external shocks, the development of the fiscal crisis and the difficulties to promote the reduction of inflation. The second part analyses the impact of the macroeconomic crisis on the major labour market variables and the distribution of income. Finally, based on the results of the models presented in Chapters 3 and 4, we study the movements of the indexation factors of wages and prices, and of relative wages and relative prices in the industrial sector.

External Adjustment and Macroeconomic Disarray

The External Adjustment

During the 1970s the Brazilian economy grew at an average rate of

7% per year. However, the environment in which such a 'miraculous' performance occurred changed dramatically towards the end of the decade, and certainly worsened in the 1980s. Adverse terms of trade shocks in 1974 and 1978–9 led to a fragile balance of payment situation considerably worsened in the early 1980s by the surge of international interest rates and the strategy of the Brazilian government to keep up with a bold investment programme intended to reduce the dependency of the economy with respect to imports of capital and intermediary goods. Such a programme relied heavily on external borrowing on the part of the private sector and state enterprises. In a sense, the growth-cum-debt strategy resulted from the necessity of the government of legitimizing the authoritarian bias of the military regime.

In the early 1980s, the Mexican moratorium led the private banks to interrupt the flow of voluntary funds to highly indebted countries which obviously meant a drastic change of regime for the Brazilian strategy. The recession of 1981–3, the import substitution process of the late 1970s and an aggressive programme of incentives to increase exports, led to a strong trade balance position from 1984 onwards. This was certainly the positive side of the adjustment – an adjustment characterized by an important change in the trade regime and the extraordinary growth of exports.

The Brazilian response to the oil shocks of 1974 and 1978 was faster growth and a deepening of the import substitution process together with an aggressive approach to export promotion. After growing at high rates during the 1970s, imports as a proportion of GDP decreased steadily after 1980. Indeed, the import propensity fell from approximately 11% in 1980 to only 5% in 1989. Exports on the other hand, although more volatile, grew in comparison to the 1970s, reaching almost 14% of GDP in 1984, and then declining. As a result, during the 1980s, trade surpluses fluctuated between 3% and 6% of GDP reaching an average of $US15 billions.

Import repression – through the reduction in absorption in 1981–3 and extremely heavy tariff and non-tariff protection – and export promotion – through different types of fiscal incentives and a real devaluation of the cruzeiro in 1983 – were responsible for the outstanding response of the trade balance. Looking at the trade balance, there is no doubt that the Brazilian economy went through a significant macroeconomic adjustment.

The consequences on the internal front, however, were far from irrelevant. Indeed, they are at the root of the current economic crisis. Foreign borrowing was an important factor in the deepening of the import substitution process in the 1970s and early 1980s. The surge of the international interest rates led to an increase of 100% of the external debt in five years. The debt went from $US54 billion in 1980 to $US102 billion in 1986. Interests on the debt went from an average of $US3 billion in the second half of the 1970s to $US9 billion in the second half of the 1980s.

The Fiscal Crisis

The fiscal crisis of the State in Brazil results, on the one hand, from the interrelation between the growth of the external debt and the fiscal debt, and on the other, from the development of clientelistic practices within the State. The relation between the fiscal crisis and the macroeconomic crisis of the late 1980s and early 1990s cannot be overstated.

Public operational savings (primary savings plus real interest on the domestic public debt) went from an average of 7% of GDP in the 1970s to around 1% in the 1980s. The government current expenditures as a percentage of GDP increased in the second half of the 1980s, specially at the state and municipal levels. These figures imply that after paying for wages and current goods and services (government consumption), the government was gradually left with a smaller share of GDP for infrastructure investment and social expenditures. In the last three years of the 1980s, the government had to borrow from the private sector to pay for its payroll and current consumption. The same is true in the case of state and local governments which, in many cases, could not even cover payroll expenses with tax revenues, and had to borrow from the private sector to pay for current consumption expenditures.

As a result of the reduction in public saving, public investment fell from 11% of GDP in 1980 to around 5% of GDP in the second half of the 1980s. The fiscal debt started increasing in the late 1970s, reaching 4% in the early 1980s and more than 6% in 1989. The causes of the reduction in the government saving and increase in the debt are essentially the following: the surge in interest on the government domestic and external debts; the reduction in gross tax revenues in the late 1980s; the increase in subsidies and the increase in government employment at the federal and state and local levels which resulted in a rapid growth of payroll expenses. The increase in the external debt resulted, on the one hand, from the borrowing of the state enterprises and the state governments, and on the other, from the absorption of private debt by the Central Bank.[1] Even more important than the amount of registered public debt and private debt absorbed by the Central Bank is the so-called 'internal transfer problem' linking the service of the external debt to the growth of the domestic government debt. In order to service the external debt the government has to buy hard currency from the export sector thus leading to an increase in either the supply of money or the issuing of public debt. Hence, the increase in the government domestic debt is directly affected by the servicing of the external debt.

The other three causes of the fiscal difficulties of the Brazilian government are in some sense associated with the nature of the political process and the particular type of relationship established between the State and the society. Clientelism have for a long time been pervasive characteristics of the Brazilian State. The structure of subsidies, for instance, has been designed to create incentives to expand exports and attenuate regional discrepancies. However, the distribution of subsidies is in many cases dictated by political kinship which obviously distorts the primary objectives of the programmes. The reduction in indirect taxation is universally seen as an instrument to reduce distributive inequities if replaced by more direct taxation. The increase in direct taxation, however, hurts the interests of powerful groups with strong political representation in Congress, and this is probably the reason why it has been so difficult to enlarge the tax base in Brazil. Finally, the number of civil servants has been swelling and there is clear evidence that clientelistic practices (nepotism and favouritism for example) have dominated the recruitment process in the public sector.

All these reasons account for a fiscal crisis in the State in Brazil which has two direct consequences. On the one hand, it strongly affects the dynamics of inflation and reduces the prospects of implementing a successful stabilization programme. On the other, it implies drastic budget cuts with important consequences on the government capacity to invest.

From a macroeconomic perspective, the 1980s in Brazil had two markedly different phases. In the first, from 1981 to mid-1984, the focus of the economic policy was the re-establishment of the external balance, especially after the Mexican moratorium and the interruption of the flows of external capital. The response to the external crunch was a drastic reduction in the level of absorption and a partially real devaluation. The policy was successful in creating substantial trade surpluses. The side effects of the strategy were the usual ones: the rate of GDP growth plunged, idle capacity increased and real wages fell.

However, the sequels of the policy adopted in 1981–3 were not only the usual and transitory ones. In a sense, the effects were felt over the decade and spilled over into the 1990s. The attempt to change relative prices through the maxi-devaluation of 1983 combined with the growing bargaining power of unions in the tradable sectors led to a typical wage–price spiral. The intensification of indexation mechanisms in the determination of wages and prices introduced a hysteresis element in the inflationary process. Between 1982 and 1984 inflation doubled, reaching 200% per year.

In 1984–5 the economy showed signs of vigorous recovery. The acceleration of inflation and the rapid increase in labour militancy led President Sarney to adopt a price freeze. With the first heterodox plan in 1986, the Cruzado Plan, a new phase began in the history of the economic policy in Brazil. The plan was very successful in reducing inflation for roughly six to eight months but it led to such a transformation in the regime of incomes formation that very rapidly it became unsustainable.[2] After the Cruzado Plan, three other 'heterodox' attempts to promote stabilization failed. A new type of inflationary regime started with the Cruzado and the following plans: the expectation or anticipation of a new freeze led firms and unions to overindex prices and wages, which obviously promoted the acceleration of inflation. Spurs of explosive inflation and price freezes marked the second half of the 1980s.

The Response of the Labour Market

The labour market responded to the macroeconomic crisis with relative stability of the employment structure, intense instability of real wages and incomes and significant changes in relative wages

156

and prices.

Figure 7.1 shows the growth rate of GDP between 1970 and 1990. The 1970s were marked by incredibly high rates of economic growth, averaging more than 7% of GDP growth and reaching 14% in 1973. The 1980s were characterized by negative growth rates in 1981 and 1983 (and zero growth in 1982) and relatively high rates in 1984–9 with the exception of 1988.

The Structure of Employment

The level of employment grew continually over the decade (Figure 7.2) from around 40 million to roughly 56 million in 1990. Open unemployment did increase during the recession, reaching almost 5% of the labour force in 1983 but then recovered very fast falling to less than 2.5% during the Cruzado, and then levelling out to around 3.5% between 1987 and 1989 (Figure 7.3). Even during the recession of 1981–3, the rate of unemployment was very small considering the negative rates of growth of GDP.

The structure of employment between wage earners with a legal contract (formal segment of the labour market) and without a legal contract, and between wage earners and self-employed did change over the decade (Figures 7.4 and 7.5). The ratio between wage workers with a legal contract and those without a legal contract fell between 1984–5 and the end of the decade, and started increasing in 1990 with the new recession. The ratio between self-employed workers and legal wage workers remained stable over the decade, and increased in the early 1990s.

These figures show that job creation was not really a problem during the 1980s. The level of employment grew approximately 35% during 10 years. There was an increase in the level of employment in the informal sector but the share of informal employment decreased.

Figure 7.6 shows the evolution of the duration of unemployment and the frequency of unemployment. The former, which measures the average number of months during which the unemployed remained unemployed, was comparatively higher during the years of recession (1983–4) then falling during the decade. It reached the minimum value in 1986 during the Cruzado Plan. In 1990, with the recession during the first year of the Collor government, it increased again. The frequency of unemployment measures the

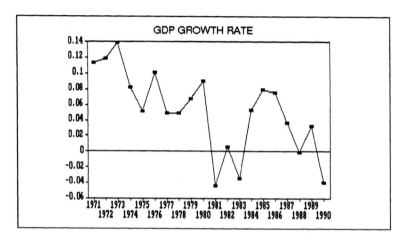

Figure 7.1

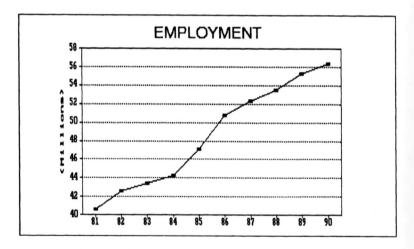

Figure 7.2

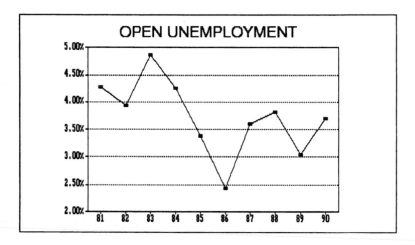

Figure 7.3

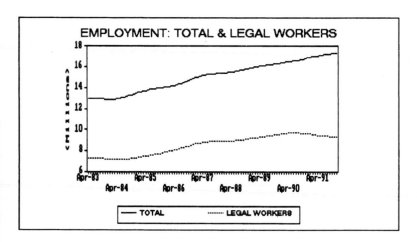

Figure 7.4

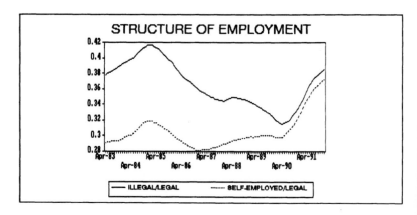

Figure 7.5

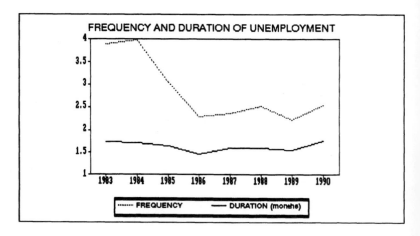

Figure 7.6

number of times a worker becomes unemployed during a year. The duration of unemployment is greater than 2 during the whole decade. It reaches almost 4 in 1983–4 and then falls gradually. It is interesting to note that the frequency of unemployment does not increase as much as the duration of unemployment in 1990. Maybe the reason for this is that the cost of firing increased considerably in 1988, with the new Constitution.

Inflation, Real Wages and Distribution

The path of annual inflation between 1970 and 1990 in Brazil is really impressive. Figure 7.7 shows that until 1978–9 the rate of annual inflation was very low (around 20%). It accelerated to 100% in 1979–80 after the second oil shock and the maxi-devaluation of 1979. It then doubled, reaching 200% in 1983–4 after the second devaluation in 1983. In the second half of the decade the rate of inflation exploded and oscillated widely. Of course, the rapid acceleration of inflation is a potent instrument of income redistribution.

The recession of 1981–3 led a reduction in the level of real income of all participants of the labour market (Figure 7.8). Legal wage earners – among whom are the more organized and militant labour groups – suffered with the recession but the reduction in their incomes was not as deep as that of the self-employed and the illegal wage workers (Figure 7.8).

The Cruzado Plan was a period of intense income redistribution in favour of the less organized labour groups whose wages and incomes are more sensitive to the cycle and are not subject to close scrutiny during price and wage freezes. The real income of all groups increased very fast in 1985–6 – roughly 40%. During the Cruzado Plan (1986) in particular, the ratio of the income of the self-employed to the income of the legal workers increased 50% and the ratio of the wage of the illegal wage workers to the wage of the legal wage earners increased 15%.

The reduction in the level of real incomes of the employed workers fell approximately 20% between 1986 and 1988 and then stabilized in 1988–90. The ratio of the income of the self-employed to the income of the legal workers fell during this period. The ratio of the income of the illegal wage earners to the income of the legal workers remained practically stable after the Cruzado Plan.

161

Figure 7.7

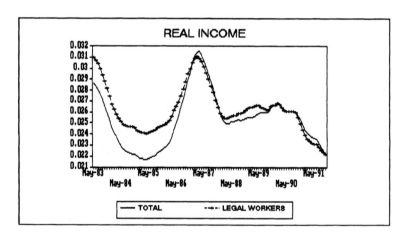

Figure 7.8

162

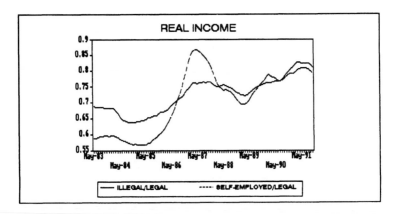

Figure 7.9

Approximately 50% of the labour force in Brazil earn less than two minimum wages, approximately $US150. The real minimum wage (Figure 7.9) fell dramatically between 1986 and 1989. The acceleration of inflation and the low degree of indexation of the minimum wage is responsible for a reduction of more than 75% of the minimum real wage between 1986 and 1989 and of approximately 70% between the average minimum real wage during the 1970s and 1989.

Bargaining Power, Mark-up Power, and Wage Differentials

As already noted in Chapter 6, in Brazil, the coordinating capability of the government in the formation of wages and prices had been gradually eroded during the 1980s. The rapid acceleration of inflation over the decade was the result of a conflict over the distribution of income involving the government, firms and workers. The government participated in this conflict in two different, but connected, instances. On the one hand, in trying to

163

adjust the economy to the external debt crisis, the two major devaluations of the domestic currency in 1979 and 1983 created obvious inflationary pressures. On the other hand, in the face of the interrelation between the rate of inflation and the government debt (due to the indexation of public bonds), the Treasury and the Central Bank had to finance the debt recurrently either by increasing money supply or issuing new bonds, thus limiting the flexibility of the government to conduct monetary and fiscal policies.

Agents in the private sector, in turn, respond to supply shocks and growing uncertainty over the path of future inflation by trying to protect their income through wage and price increases. The loss of control over macroeconomic variables led the government in March 1986 (and again in 1987, 1989, 1990 and 1991) to adopt the heterodox programmes. However, these plans have all failed. Private agents simply did not respect the freeze of wages and prices.

So far, stabilization attempts have failed in Brazil, and it is the hypothesis of this chapter that the stabilization crisis is not independent of institutional and economic factors affecting the attitude of unions in wage bargains. It is the objective of the chapter to examine the factors accounting for the determination of wages (and prices) in economies with chronic and accelerating inflationary processes, and to access the role played by unions and wage bargaining in the specific case of Brazil.

The Argument Re-stated

In what follows we re-write the main equations of the model developed in Chapters 2 and 3, and briefly re-state the main concepts and arguments concerning the determinants of wages in economies with high and chronic inflation.

We assume that firms fix a mark-up over direct average costs. The size of the mark-up varies with structural factors (such as barriers to entry, monopoly rights, protection from international competition) as well as short-run fluctuations (such as movements in the elasticity of demand). Firms have both direct labour and non-labour costs, and in each sector the weight of each of them in total direct costs varies. The price equation of a typical firm j is given by:[3]

$$\Pi_j = M_j[(W_j / \Delta_j)^\gamma * (\Pi \beta_j)^{1-\gamma}] \qquad (2.11)$$

The time derivative of this equations yields the rate of inflation of the price of good j:

$$\pi_j = m_j + c_j \qquad (2.12)$$

Price inflation can also be written as:

$$\pi_j = \epsilon_j c_j \qquad (2.13)$$

From equations (2.1) and (2.1) it is clear that whenever the indexation factor ϵ_j is greater than 1, the mark-up increases (that is $m_j > 0$) and vice-versa. The ratio of price inflation of two firms j and k is obviously given by:

$$\pi_j / \pi_k = (\epsilon_j / \epsilon_k)(c_j / c_k) \qquad (7.1)$$

where the ratio (ϵ_j/ϵ_k) measures the relative mark-up power of firms j and k.

When negotiating money wages, unions attempt to recover the purchasing power losses of wages incurred due to inflation since the last bargain. In addition, they bargain over 'real increases' in wages due to changes in labour productivity. We assume that changes in money wages in sector j are given by the following equation:

$$w_j = \lambda_j(p + \xi_j) \qquad (2.8)$$

Note that whenever $\lambda_j > 1$, given the rate of inflation, *real* wages will grow faster than productivity in which case we say that there is 'overindexation' of wages. The path of relative wages over time, given by

$$w_j \, / w_k = (\lambda_j \, / \lambda_k)[(p+ \xi_j)/(p+ \xi_k)] \qquad (7.2)$$

depends on the path of labour productivity in the two firms and on the relative bargaining power of the respective unions.

The inflationary process and the associated distributional implications are critically influenced by the sizes of the indexation factors of industrial prices with respect to costs (ε) and of money wages with respect to the consumer price and productivity (λ). Equation (2.8) shows quite clearly that the rate of inflation of industrial prices is positively influenced by the size of these two indexation factors. The acceleration of inflation results necessarily from the overindexation of wages and/or prices.

As seen in the previous chapters, there are a variety of elements, different in nature, affecting the bargaining attitude of unions in wage negotiations. Institutions, market constraints and expectations are all important factors. The central notion, however, is that unions and workers care about the future path of relative wages when bargaining over their wages. This notion was first put forward by Keynes in the *General Theory*. In Keynes's view, the average real wage depends on the aggregate rate of inflation over which individual unions do not have any control. On the other hand, the distribution of the aggregate wage bill among workers of different sectors depends on the path of relative wages. As the level of centralization of bargains increases, unions may start to have a sense of the likely effect of their wage demands on aggregate variables. If this is indeed the case, the incentives to overindex money wages in each bargaining party, in an attempt to increase the relative wage of the union members, are reduced as the level of centralization of wage bargaining increases. In principle, the greater the size of the bargaining party, the more stringent becomes the trade-off between the direct positive effect on the relative wage of the workers involved in the negotiation and the indirect negative effect over their real wage due to the rise in inflation resulting from the overindexation of money wages.

The length of time over which wage contracts are binding is also important in determining the attitude of unions. Here, it is important to distinguish between two types of periods. First, the time lapse between two wage bargains, say one or two years. Second, the time interval after which wages are automatically adjusted to inflation as a result of a legal or negotiated wage policy, say every three or six months. On the one hand, the longer the period between negotiations, the greater the lack of relevant information concerning the likely path of inflation, and thus the greater the incentives on the part of unions to take preemptive action to prevent a reduction in the real wage. On the other hand, the effect over the real wage of an unexpected acceleration of inflation is stronger the longer the period of automatic wage adjustment. Workers' militancy, and hence the incentives to demand overindexation of wages, tends to be positively correlated to the length of both types of periods for the likelihood of windfall real wage losses grows as the periods become longer.

Market conditions, both at the aggregate level and at the sectoral level, affect the net bargaining power of unions and firms. In a situation of growing aggregate demand for labour, the bargaining power of unions increases thus inducing wage overindexation. On the other hand, the goods market poses a constraint for the individual firm which will resist increases in wage costs. Hence, the greater the market constraint, the greater the willingness of the firm to resist wage increases, and to impose conflict costs on unions.

The goods and labour markets at the sectoral level have their own dynamics but they certainly interact. The attitude of firms in wage bargains is affected by the goods market constraint they face. Given the market constraint, the willingness of a firm or group of firms to impose conflict costs on workers grows with the demand for wage increases. If, for example, the firm chooses to peg the price to the rate of inflation in the international market, given the path of labour productivity and of non-labour costs, there is an obvious trade-off between the indexation of wages (λ) and the indexation of the price (ε). The actual levels of λ and ε will depend on the incentives to the union to overindex wages and the relative bargaining power of the union and the firm.

The alleviation of the goods market constraint, say by an acceleration of inflation of the relevant price in the international market, reduces the pressures over the profit margin of wage increases and, as a result, mitigates the willingness of the firm to impose conflict costs on workers. Firms become more tolerant and workers have an extra incentive to demand wage increases as market conditions become more favourable. As a result, it seems plausible to assume that both the indexation factors of wages and prices will tend to increase. This argument implies that, to the extent that market conditions are an important determinant of the bargaining structure between the union and the firm, the indexation factors of wages and prices will tend to move together over time. By the same reasoning, the path of the relative bargaining power between unions in two firms (λ_j/λ_k) will tend to move together with the path of the relative mark-up power between the corresponding firms $(\varepsilon_j/\varepsilon_k)$.

When inflation is high and accelerating, agents stop looking to the past and start looking to the future in order to determine their wages and prices. They form expectations concerning the evolution of the relevant inflation for each one of them, and try to fix their prices accordingly. The disparity between expectations and between the market power of agents induces an increase in the dispersion of the indexation factors of prices and wages as inflation accelerates.

However, there seem to exist countervailing forces acting in the opposite direction. In the particular case of countries with chronic and unstable inflation, the adherence of wages to the official wage policy depends on such factors as the rate of unemployment, the degree of centralization of the union movement and of the wage bargaining process, and on the period of wage indexation. A high rate of unemployment tames the incentives to overindex wages and hence increases the adherence of wages to the wage policy, reducing wage drift. The centralization of the union movement leads to greater homogeneity of the bargaining power of sectoral or local unions while the centralization of wage bargains reduces the discrepancies between wage demands. Finally, the shorter the period of (automatic) wage adjustment, the smaller the risk for the workers of experiencing windfall losses due to unexpected inflationary surges, and thus the smaller the incentives to overindex wages. Unions which otherwise would demand and obtain greater wage adjustments, thus increasing wage dispersion, have less incentive to do so when the period of adjustment is short.

An Empirical Evaluation of the Brazilian Case

As noted in Chapter 6, in Brazil, the incentives to overindexation of wages are enormous. Wage bargains are decentralized, which implies that unions are exclusively concerned with the relative wage of their members. However, over the last ten years, negotiations have become more centralized *within* industries. As a result, union leaders still do not care about the reverberation of wage demands on inflation but have increased their bargaining power as a result of the clustering of unions. The fact that the Brazilian economy is remarkably closed and that, with the exception of one short period (1981–3), the government has conducted a very accommodative monetary policy, are also important elements in explaining the high incidence of overindexation. Finally, the continuous expectation that inflation will accelerate in the future provides yet additional incentives to demand overindexation. Needless to say, these expectations are, in a sense, self-fulfilling.

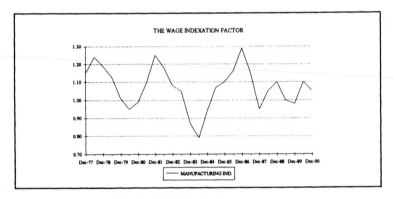

Figure 7.10

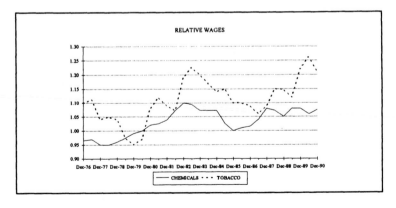

Figure 7.11

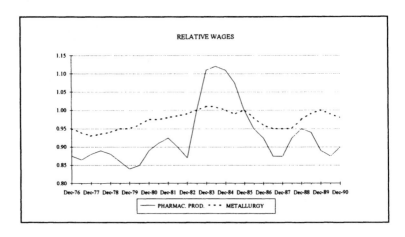

Figure 7.12

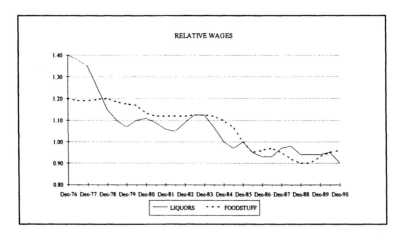

Figure 7.13

Figure 7.10 and column 3 in Table 7.1 provide evidence of wage overindexation in Brazil.[4] Figure 7.10 shows the movement of the

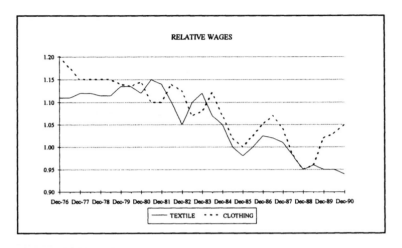

RELATIVE WAGES

Figure 7.14

12 months moving average of λ in the industrial sector as a whole. The indexation factor of wages is calculated by dividing the annual rate of wage inflation by the sum of the annual rate of CPI inflation and the proportional change in labour productivity. With the exception of two very short periods in 1987 and 1988, and the recession of 1982–3, the indexation factor of wages is greater than 1, implying that over most of the period, money wages grew faster than past CPI inflation plus labour productivity.

The figures in column 3 in Table 7.1 provide a measure of overindexation for the manufacturing sectors. This measure is the sum, over the period 1976–90, of $\lambda - 1$, that is, $\Sigma \ (\lambda_t - 1)$ over t. With the exception of only one sector (liquors), the measure of overindexation is positive, indicating that the incidence of overindexation is considerably greater than that of underindexation.

It is not surprising that the sectors for which the measures of overindexation are greater are also the ones in which relative wages grew over the period. Columns 1 and 2 in Table 7.1 display the structure of wage differentials in 1976 and 1991. Wage differentials are measured by the ratio of the wage in the specific sector to the average wage in industry.

Column 1 in Table 7.2 provides a measure of the relative bargaining power in each sector. The measure of relative bargaining power in column 3 is calculated as follows:

$$RBP_j = \Sigma_t(\frac{\lambda_{j,t}}{\lambda_t} - 1)$$

where λ_t is the average indexation factor. With a few exceptions, those sectors in which wages were greater than the average in 1976 were the same in which the relative bargaining power were positive and relative wages grew over the period 1976–91. Figures 7.11 to 7.14 show the movement in relative wages in four sectors in the Brazilian industry. Figures 7.11 and 7.12 depict the cases of the chemical and tobacco and pharmaceutical products and metallurgy industries, respectively, where relative wages grew between the mid-1970s and the late 1980s. Figures 7.13 and 7.14 portray the cases of the liquors and foodstuff and textile and clothing industries, respectively, where relative wages fell. To explore the factors determining the movement of the relative bargaining power, we look at the movement of the relative mark-up power $\varepsilon_j/\varepsilon_k$ (column 2 in Table 7.2) and the correlation between the measures of relative bargaining and mark-up power in each sector (column 3 in Table 7.2). We note that, with the exception of four sectors, the correlation between the measures is positive.

This result may be interpreted as an indication that sectoral market conditions, which have a direct effect on the mark-up power of firms, also have an indirect effect on the behaviour of the bargaining power of the corresponding unions. As noted above, firms are more tolerant and workers have an extra incentive to demand wage increases in sectors in which market conditions are more favourable. Indeed, the sectors in which relative wages grew have, on average, a much greater degree of industrial concentration (column 4) and are the sectors which have received government incentives (export subsidies and protection from external competition) over the period under consideration. Also, they are undoubtedly the sectors in which the labour movement is best organized. A last piece of evidence on the behaviour of the relative bargaining power measure refers to its dispersion over time. In spite of the acceleration of inflation, as seen in Figure 7.15, dispersion

Table 7.1 Relative wages and bargaining power

	Relative wages*		$\Sigma(\lambda_j - 1)$
	1976	1991	
	(1)	(2)	
Sectors			
Growing relative wages			
Mechanic	1.51	1.59	13.6
Chemicals	1.43	1.65	9.2
Transport equipment	1.32	1.39	16.3
Electrical material	1.04	1.21	11.7
Pharmaceutical	1.01	1.13	19.2
Mineral extraction	1.00	1.57	15.5
Metallurgy	1.05	1.21	11.9
Rubber	0.75	0.98	16.4
Tobacco	0.64	0.85	6.8
Paper	0.80	0.85	7.8
Falling relative wages			
Perfumes, etc.	1.01	0.85	1.5
Plastic materials	1.09	0.82	5.0
Liquors	1.15	0.77	–0.7
Textile	0.76	0.70	7.5
Process	0.73	0.65	6.8
Foodsuff	0.71	0.61	9.4
Clothing	0.55	0.54	10.5

Source: Pesquisa Industrial Mensal, IBGE.
* Wage differentials are measured by the ratio of the wage in the specific sector to the average wage in industry.

Table 7.2 Bargaining power and mark-up power

Conc[b]	$\sum[(\lambda_r/\lambda) - 1]$	$\sum[(\varepsilon_r/\varepsilon) - 1]$	Corr[a]	Ind.
Growing relative wages				
Mechanic	2.42	4.80	0.25[+2]	13.4
Chemicals	1.17	-7.00	0.64[-3]	48.2
Transport equipment	5.28	8.00	-0.38[-3]	55.4
Electrical material	0.13	-3.00	0.11[-3]	54.7
Pharmaceutical	5.54	0.90	0.26[+3]	25.5
Mineral extraction	6.47	1.20	0.38[+2]	83.1
Metallurgy	2.36	6.70	0.57[-3]	35.1
Rubber	6.62	3.24	0.26[+3]	67.3
Tobacco	-0.87	8.90	-0.59[-3]	83.8
Paper	-1.31	9.17	-0.46[-3]	29.1
Falling relative wages				
Perfumes, etc	-8.07	-0.21	0.33[+3]	52.3
Plastic materials	-3.73	-4.40	0.24[+3]	17.5
Liquors	-7.39	1.04	-0.51[+3]	33.5
Textile	-1.56	-5.50	0.28[+3]	14.8
Process	-1.97	-4.32	0.13[-3]	16.2
Foodsuff	0.32	0.81	0.75[+3]	11.9
Clothing	1.43	9.50	0.36[+3]	12.2

Notes

[a] Correlation between λ_r/λ and $\varepsilon_r/\varepsilon$. The figures in parenthesis indicate the lag [-] or lead [+] of λ_r/λ in which the highest correlation with $\varepsilon_r/\varepsilon$ was observed.

[b] Industrial concentration: percentage share of the gross value of the industrial production of the largest eight firms in the sector.

Source: Pesquisa Industrial Mensal, IBGE. Relative wages.

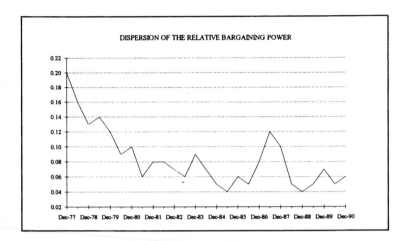

Figure 7.15

as measured by the standard deviation of λ fell over the period. We impute the decline to the gradual reduction of the adjustment period of wages and prices as inflation accelerated. As mentioned above, as the adjustment period shrinks, the incentive for unions to demand overindexation is reduced, thus lessening the dispersion of the relative bargaining power. The centralization of the union movement during the 1980s enhanced the bargaining power of the weaker unions, thus contributing to the reduction in the dispersion. The increase in dispersion in 1986–7 is associated with the first (and longest) price freeze when the process of coordination of wages became quite inoperative.

Concluding Notes

The determinants of the mark-up power of firms and bargaining power of unions seem crucial for understanding certain important aspects of inflationary processes. Institutions, market structures and expectations are all relevant in this connection. The uncertainty concerning the future path of inflation and the lack of effective coordinating instruments (such as a wage policy or 'pattern setters') in the formation of wages and prices, generate incentives to overindexation. High degrees of protection against external competition and industrial concentration, on the one hand, and the repeated adoption of an accommodative monetary policy, on the other, reduce the degree of market restrictions which restricts the appetite to raise prices and wages.

In Brazil, the coordinating instruments in the formation of wages and prices were gradually eroded over the 1980s. The decentralization of wage bargains and the expectation of accelerating inflation led the unions to assume a very aggressive attitude. The process of political democratization over the decade helped to increase the bargaining power of the unions. The only factor with a positive effect over coordination was the shortening of the indexation period of wages, which reduced the anxiety of the unions and the incentives to overindexation. A series of frustrated price and wage freezes, after 1986, gave rise to a new inflationary regime. The uncertainty no longer referred to the possibility of inflationary shocks only, but to the adoption of a new freeze. The expectation of a new freeze leads to preemptive actions on the part of agents to avoid being caught in an adverse position. This obviously increased the tension between unions and employers.

The experience so far has demonstrated that price and wage controls are quite ineffective in Brazil. The institutional apparatus on which wages are negotiated (decentralized bargaining), the structural features of the economy (highly protected industry, in particular), and the uncertainty concerning the eventuality of a new 'policy shock' (that is, a new freeze) seem to be at the root of the stabilization crisis and the government's inability to coordinate the formation of wages and prices.

Notes

1. The decision to absorb the private external debt was intended to protect private borrowers from the exchange rate and interest rate shocks. In reducing the risk of the private borrowers, the government implicitly socialized the debt.
2. For an analysis of the distributive effects of the plans and the causes of the failure, see Camargo and Ramos (1988) and Amadeo and Camargo (1988).
3. Refer to Chapters 2 and 3 for the notation. The time subscripts have been omitted for simplicity.

4. The source of the data is the *Monthly Industrial Survey* conducted by the Brazilian Institute of Statistics and Geography (IBGE).

References

Amadeo, E. (1986), 'Notes on Distribution, Accumulation and Capacity utilization', in *Contributions to Political Economy*.

Amadeo, E. (1991a), 'Bargaining power, mark-up power and the acceleration of inflation in Brazil (1976–85)', *Discussion Paper*, Department of Economics, PUC/RJ.

Amadeo, E. (1991b), 'The rational basis of wage determination in regimes of high inflation' (mimeo), Department of Economics, University of Notre Dame.

Amadeo, E. (1993), 'Restricciones institucionales a la politica economica: negociacion salarial y estabilizacion en Brazil', *Desarrollo Economico*, vol. 33, no. 129, Buenos Aires.

Amadeo, E. and Banuri, T. (1991), 'Policy, government and the management of conflict', in Banuri, T. (ed.), *No Panacea: the limits of economic liberalization*, Oxford University Press. Reprinted in Spanish (1989), *El trimestre Economico*.

Amadeo, E. and Camargo, J.M. (1988) 'Choque e Concerto', *Revista Dados*, Rio de Janeiro.

Amadeo, E. and Camargo, J.M. (1992), 'Uma análise Estruturalista da Inflação e da Estabilização', *Revista de Economia Política*.

Amadeo, E. and Estevão, M. (1994), *A teoria econômica do desemprego*, Hucitec, São Paulo.

Aguirre, M.B. et al. (1985), *A trajetória das negociações coletivas de trabalho nos anos 1980*, Ministério do Trabalho, Brasília.

Arida, P. and Lara Rezende, A. (1985), 'Inertial inflation and monetary reform in Brazil', in Williamson, J. (ed.), *Inflation and Indexation in Argentina, Brazil and Israel*, MIT Press, Cambridge.

Bacha, E. (1987), 'A inércia e o conflito: o Plano Cruzado e seus desafios', *Discussion Paper*, no. 133, Department of Economics, PUC/RJ.

Bacha, E. (1982), 'Análise macroeconômica: um texto intermediário', IPEA/INPES, Rio de Janeiro.

Baglioni, G. (1987), 'Constants and variants in political exchange', *Labour*, vol. 1, no. 3, pp. 57–94.

Bell, L. and Freeman, R. (1987), 'Flexible wage structures and employment', in Gunderson, M. et al. (eds), *Unemployment:*

References

international comparisons, University of Toronto Press.

Bhaduri, A. and Marglin, S. (1987), 'Conflict, cooperation and unemployment' (mimeo), WIDER/UNU.

Bilson, B. (1987), *Wage Restraint and the control of inflation*, Croom Helm.

Blanchard, O. and Summers, L. (1986), 'Hysteresis and the European economic problem', in *NBER Macroeconomics Annual*, MIT Press, Cambridge.

Blanpain, R. (1987), 'Belgium', in Windmuller, J. (ed.), *Collective Bargaining in industrialized market economies: a reappraisal*, ILO, Geneve.

Bowles, S. and Boyler, L. (1987), 'Income distribution, labour discipline, and unemployment' (mimeo), WIDER/UNU.

Bruno, M. (1988), 'Econometrics and the design of economic reform', p. 52, *NBER Working Paper*, no. 2718, NBER, Massachusetts.

Bruno, M. and Sachs, J. (1985), *Economics of Worldwide Stagflation*, Harvard University Press.

Buchanan, P. (1989), 'Plus ça change? A administração nacional do trabalho e a democracia no Brasil, 1985–87', *Revista Dados*.

Cacciamalli, M. (1991), 'As economias informal e submersa: conceitos e distribuição de renda', in Camargo, J.M. e Giambiagi, F. (orgs.), *A distribuição de renda no Brasil*, Paz e Terra, Rio de Janeiro.

Caire, G. (1987), 'France', in Windmuller, J. (ed.), *Collective Bargaining in industrialized market economies: a reappraisal*, ILO, Geneve.

Calmfors, L. (1985), 'Trade unions, wage formation and macroeconomic stability: an introduction', *The Scandinavian Journal of Economics*, vol. 87, no. 2.

Calmfors, L and Driffill, J. (1988), 'Centralization of Wage Bargaining', *Economic Policy*, no. 6.

Calmfors, L. and Horn, H. (1985), 'Classical unemployment, accommodation policies and the adjustment of real wage', *The Scandinavian Journal of Economics*, vol. 87, no. 2.

Camargo, J.M. (1990), 'Salários e negociações coletivas', *Discussion Paper*, no. 244, Department of Economics, PUC-RJ.

Camargo, J.M. (1988), 'Ativismo sindical, inflação e o congelamento' (mimeo), PREAL/OIT.

Camargo, J.M. and Ramos, C.A. (1988), *A Revolução Indesejada*,

179

Campus, Rio de Janeiro.
Cameron, D. (1985), 'Social democracy, corporatism, labour quiescence, and the representation of economic interest in advanced capitalist society', in Goldthorpe, J. (ed.), *Order and conflict in contemporary capitalism*, Clarendon Press, Oxford.
Carrieri, M. and Donolo, C. (1987), 'The political party as a problem for the trade unions in Italy: 1975–83', *Labour*, vol. 1, no. 1, pp.129–46.
CLACSO (1985), *El sindicalismo latinoamericano en los ochenta*, CLACSO, Santiago.
Collier, R. and Collier, D. (1979), 'Inducements versus constraints: disaggregating corporatism', *The American Political Science Review*, vol. 73, no. 4.
Costa, A. (1986), *Estado e controle sindical no Brasil*, T.A. Queiroz, São Paulo.
Cotta, L. (1989), 'Construção dos índices das greves ocorridas no período 1983–87', Undergraduate dissertation, Department of Economics, PUC-RJ.
Crouch, C. (1978), 'Inflation and the political organization of political interests', in Hirsch, F. and Golthorpe, J. (eds), *The political economy of inflation*, Harvard University Press.
Crouch, C. (1985a), 'Conditions for trade union and wage restraint', in Lindberg, L. and Maier, C. (eds), *The economics of inflation and economic stagnation*, Brookings Institution, Washington.
Crouch, C. (1985b), 'Corporatism in industrial relations: a formal model', in Grant, W. (ed.), *The political economy of corporatism*, Macmillan, London.
Dutt, A.K. (1984), 'Stagnation, income distribution and monopoly power', *Cambridge Journal of Economics*, vol. 8.
Dutt, A.K. (1987), 'Alternative Closures Again: comments on "Growth, Distribution and Inflation"', *Cambridge Journal of Economics*, vol. 10.
Dutt, A. (1990), *Growth, distribution and uneven development*, Cambridge University Press.
Epstein, E. (ed.) (1989), *Labor autonomy and the state in Latin America*, Unwin Hyman, New York.
Esping-Andersen, G. and Korpi, W. (1985), 'Social policy as class politics in post-war capitalism: Scandinavia, Austria, and Germany', in Goldthorpe, J. (ed.), *Order and conflict in contemporary capitalism*, Clarendon Press, Oxford.

References

Filgueira, C. 'Organizaciones sindicales y empresariales ante las politicas de estabilizacion: Uruguay, 1985–87' (mimeo), PREALC.

Flanagan et al. (1983), *Unionism, economic stabilization and incomes policies: European experience*, Brookings Institution, Washington.

Franco, G. (1987), 'Inertia, coordination and corporatism', Discussion Paper, Department of Economics, PUC/RJ.

Frankel, R. (1979), 'Decisiones de precio en alta inflacion', *Estudios CEDES*, CEDES, Buenos Aires.

Frankel, R. and Damill, M. (1988), 'Concertacion y politica de ingressos en Uruguay, 1985–88' (mimeo), CEDES.

Freeman, R. (1989), 'On the divergence in unionism among developed countries', *NBER Working Paper*, no. 2817.

Freeman, R. and Blanchflower, D. (1990), 'Going different ways: unionism in the US and other advanced OECD countries', *NBER Working Paper*, no. 3342.

Giugni, G. (1987), 'Social concertation and political system in Italy', *Labour*, vol. 1, no. 1, pp. 3–14.

Goldthorpe, J. (1984), *Order and conflict in contemporary capitalism*, Clarendon Press, Oxford.

Gonzaga, G. (1989), 'Efetividade da política salarial no Brasil, 1964–85', MA dissertation, Department of Economics, PUC-RJ.

Hirshman, A. (1985), 'Reflections on the Latin American experience', in Lindberg, L. and Maier, C. (eds), *The economics of inflation and economic stagnation*, Brookings Institution, Washington.

IBGE (1987), *Indicadores sociais, sindicatos*, IBGE, Rio de Janeiro.

IBGE, *Pesquisa Industrial Mensal*, IBGE, Rio de Janeiro, various issues.

IBRART (1985), *A trajetória das negociações coletivas*, IBRART, São Paulo.

ILO (1989), *Current approaches to collective bargaining*, ILO, Geneve.

Jackman, R. (1988), 'Wage formation in Nordic countries viewed from an international perspective', *Working Paper*, no. 1042, Center for Labour Economics.

Keynes, J.M. (1936), *The general theory of unemployment, interest and money*, Macmillan, London.

Klau, F. and Mittelstadt, A. (1986), 'Labour market flexibility',

181

OECD Economic Studies.

Kochan, T. and Wever, K. (1988), 'Industrial relations agenda for change: the case of the US', *Labour*, vol. 2, no. 2, pp. 21–56.

Korpi, W. and Shalev, M. (1979), 'Strikes, industrial relations and class conflict in capitalist societies', *British Journal of Sociology*, vol. 30.

Lange, P. (1981), 'The conjunctural condition for consensual wage regulation: an initial examination of some hypotheses', paper prepared for the annual meeting of the American Political Science Association, New York; cited by Katzenstein (1983).

Lange, P. (1985), 'Unions, workers, and wage regulation: the rational basis of consent', in Goldthorpe, J. (ed.), *Order and conflict in contemporary capitalism*, Clarendon Press, Oxford.

Layard, R. and Nickell, S. (1986), 'Unemployment in Britain', *Economica*, vol. 53, no. 210, pp. 121–69.

Lindbeck, A. and Snower, D.J. (1988), 'Long-term unemployment and macroeconomic policy', *American Economic Journal*, vol. 78, no. 2.

Lipietz, A. et al. (1990), 'The rise and fall of the golden age of capitalism', in Marglin, S. and Schor, J. (eds), *The golden age of capitalism*, Oxford University Press.

Lloyd, U. and Flanagan, R. (1971), *Wage restraint: a study of incomes policies in Western Europe*, University of California Press.

Lopes, F. (1984), 'Inflação inercial, hiperinflação e desinflação: notas e 'conjecturas', *Revista da ANPEC*, Rio de Janeiro.

Lopes, F. (1986), *O Choque heterodoxo*, Campus, Rio de Janeiro.

Lorenz, E.H. (1991), 'Trust, cooperation and flexibility: a framework for international comparisons' (mimeo), Department of Economics, University of Notre Dame.

Maia, R. and Saldanha, R. (1989), 'Política de salário mínimo: uma questão a ser equacionada', in Paes e Barros e Sedlaseck (orgs.), *Mercado de Trabalho e distribuição de renda*, IPEA, Rio de Janeiro.

Marglin, S. (1984), 'Growth, distribution and inflation', *Cambridge Journal of Economics*, vol. 8, no. 2.

Marglin, S. and Bhaduri, A. (1986), 'Distribution, capacity utilization and growth' (mimeo), WIDER/UNU.

Marglin, S. and Bhaduri, A. (1987), 'Profit squeeze, stagnationist models and Keynesian theory' (mimeo), WIDER/UNU.

References

Marglin, S. and Bhaduri, A. (1990), 'Profit squeeze and Keynesian Theory', in Marglin, S. and Schor, J. (eds), *The Golden Age of Capitalism*, Clarendon Press, Oxford.

Marinho, E. (1990), 'Transferência de renda dos trabalhadores do setor competitivo para o setor oligopolizado', Ph.D. dissertation, EPGE/FGV.

Martins, H.H. (1979), *O estado e a burocratização do sindicato no Brasil*, Hucitec, São Paulo.

McDonald, I. and Solow, R. (1981), 'Wage bargaining and unemployment', *American Economic Review*, vol. 71.

Meneguello, R. (1989), *PT, a formação de um partido, 1979–82*, Paz e Terra, São Paulo.

Mericle, K.S. (1974), 'Conflict Regulation in the Brazilian Industrial Relations System', Ph.D dissertation, University of Wisconsin.

Ministério do Trabalho, *Indicadores*, various issues.

Modiano, E. (1985a), 'O repasse gradual: da inflação passada aos preços futuros', *Pesquisa e Planejamento Econômico*, Rio de Janeiro.

Modiano, E. (1985b), 'Salários, preços e câmbio: os multiplicadores dos choques em uma economia indexada', *Pesquisa e Planejamento Economico*, Rio de Janeiro.

Neder, R. et al. (1988), *Automação e movimento sindical no Brasil*, Hucitec, São Paulo.

Nelson, J. (1992). 'Organized labor, politics and labor market flexibility in developing countries', *World Bank Research Observer*, Washington.

Pastore, J. and Zylberstajn, H. (1988), *A administração do conflito trabalhista no Brasil*, IPE/USP, São Paulo.

Pekkarinen, J. (1988), 'Keynesianism and the Scandinavian models of economic policy', *Working Paper*, no. 35, WIDER.

Pizzorno, A. (1978), 'Political exchange and collective identity in industrial conflict' in Crouch, C. and Pizzorno, A. (eds), *The resurgence of class conflicts in Western Europe since 1968*, Macmillan, London.

Przeworski, A. (1985), *Capitalism and social democracy*, Cambridge University Press.

Regini, M. (1985), 'The conditions for political exchange: how concertation emerged and collapsed in Italy and Britain', in Goldthorpe, J. (ed.), *Order and conflict in contemporary capitalism*, Clarendon Press, Oxford.

Robinson, J. (1939), *The economics of imperfect competition*, Macmillan, London.

Rodrigues, L.M. (1990), *CUT: os militantes e a ideologia*, Paz e Terra.

Ros, J. (1988), 'On inertia, social conflict and the structuralist analysis of inflation' (mimeo), WIDER/UNU.

Ros, J. (1989), 'A review of the literature on stabilization and inflation' (mimeo), WIDER.

Ros, J. (1991), 'Foreign exchange and fiscal constraints on growth: a reconsideration of structuralist and macroeconomic approaches' (mimeo), Department of Economics, University of Notre Dame.

Rowthorn, B. (1981), 'Demand, real wages and economic growth', *Studi Economici*.

Rowthorn, B. and Glyn, A. (1987), 'Coping with unemployment: some success stories' (mimeo), WIDER/UNU.

Rowthorn, B. and Glyn, A. (1990), 'Diversity of unemployment experiences', in Marglin, S. and Schor, J. (eds), *The golden age of capitalism*, Oxford University Press.

Sachs, J. (1979), 'Wages, profits and macroeconomic adjustment', *Brookings Papers on Economic Activity*, Washington.

Sachs, J. (1983), 'Real wages and unemployment in OECD countries', *Brookings Papers on Economic Activity*, Washington.

Sader, E. (1988), *Quando novos personagens entram em cena*, Paz e Terra, São Paulo.

Sandoval, S. (1984), 'Strikes in Brazil: 1945–80', Ph.D dissertation, University of Michigan.

Santi, E. (1988), 'Ten years of unionization in Italy', *Labour*, vol. 2, no. 1, pp. 151–81.

Santos, W.G. (1990), 'A regulamentação no Brasil', (mimeo) IUPERJ.

Schimitter, P. (1971), *Interest conflict and political change in Brazil*, Stanford University Press.

Schor, J. (1985), 'Changes in the cyclical pattern of real wages: evidence from nine countries', *Economic Journal*, vol. 95.

Shapiro, C. and Stiglitz, J.E. (1984), 'Equilibrium unemployment as a worker discipline device', American Economic Review, vol. 74, no. 3, pp. 433–44.

Shirai, T. (1987), 'Japan', in Windmuller, J. (ed.), *Collective Bargaining in industrialized market economies: a reappraisal*,

References

ILO, Geneve.

Silva, R. (org.) (1986), *Os sindicatos e a transição democrática*, IBRT, São Paulo.

Simonsen, M. (1983), 'Indexation: current theory and the Brazilian experience', in Dornbush, R. and Simonsen, M. (eds), *Inflation, debt and indexation*, MIT Press, Cambridge.

Snyder, D. (1975), 'Institutional setting and industrial conflict: comparative analysis of France, Italy and the US', *American Sociological Review*, vol. 40, no. 3.

Solow, R. (1986), 'Unemployment: getting the questions right', *Economica*.

Souza, A. (1978), 'The nature of corporatist representation: leaders and members of organized labor in Brazil', Ph.D. dissertation, MIT.

Steindl, J. (1952), *Maturity and Stagnation in American Capitalism*, Monthly Review Press, New York.

Takanashi, A. et al. (1989), 'Shunto wage offensive: historical overview and prospects', *The Japan Institute of Labour*.

Tarantelli, E. (1983), 'The regulation of inflation in western countries and the degree of neocorporatism', *Economia*, vol. 7, no. 3, pp. 199–237, Lisboa.

Tarantelli, E. (1986), *Economia politica del lavoro*, UTET, Roma.

Tarantelli, E. (1987), 'Monetary policy and the regulation of inflation and unemployment', in Gunderson, M. et al. (eds), *Unemployment: international perspectives*, University of Toronto Press.

Tavares de Almeida, M.H. (1988), 'Dificil caminho: sindicatos e política na construção da democracia', in Reis, F.W. and O'Donnell, G. (eds), *A democracia no Brasil: dilemas e perspectivas*, Vértice, São Paulo.

Tavares de Almeida, M. (1985), 'Sindicalismo brasileiro e pacto social', in CLACSO, *El sindicalismo latinoamericano en los ochenta*.

Taylor, L. (1983), *Structuralist Macroeconomics*, Basic Books, New York.

Taylor, L. (1985), 'A Stagnationist Model of Economic Growth', *Cambridge Journal of Economics*.

Taylor, L. (1987), 'The real wage, output and inflation in the Third World' (mimeo), MIT.

Taylor, L. (1991), *Income distribution, inflation and growth:*

185

lectures on structuralist macroeconomic theory, MIT Press, Cambridge.

Therborn, G. (1986), *Why some people are more unemployed than others*, Verso, New York.

Treu, T. (1987), 'Centralization and decentralization in collective bargaining', *Labour*, vol. 1, no. 1, pp. 147–75.

Vasconcellos, M. (1983), 'A ação dos sindicatos e os diferenciais de salários', Ph.D. dissertation, University of São Paulo.

Viana, L. W. (1978), *Liberalismo e sindicato no Brasil*, Paz e Terra, São Paulo.

Wallerstein, M. (1987), 'Union centralization and trade dependence: the origins of democratic corporatism' (mimeo), UCLA.

Windmuller, J. et al. (1987), *Collective bargaining in industrialized economies*, ILO, Geneve.

Index

187